Christ in the Now

Charles Reed

PO Box 188 Swartz Louisiana

For inquiries to the author or other information, correspond to Charles Reed at 701 Parkwood Drive, West Monroe, LA 71291.

For information on the Nance Publishing Company write to P.O. Box 188 Swartz, LA 71281-0188 or call (318) 343-1130. On the Internet email info@nancepub.com or visit our website www.nancepub.com.

FIRST EDITION

Cover Design by Julia Robertson Nettles II

ISBN: 1-888189-00-2

Dedication

I would like to dedicate this book to the memory of my good friend, George Donley. I met George in 1970 while I was serving as Pastor of the First Assembly of God Church in Great Bend, Kansas. George was a salesman and Sports Director at radio station KVGB, Great Bend, Kansas. During this time I started a weekly radio program at KVGB, which George Donley produced. Out of this developed a lifelong friendship.

In May of 1997, George came to work for me at Television Station, KMCT in Monroe, Louisiana. It was his suggestion that I take the radio messages that I had preached on the "Christ in the Now" radio program and make them into a book. This book is a result of that suggestion. On July 27, 1997, George went home to be with the Lord. I shall always treasure him as a dear friend.

The inspiration for the title of my radio program in the early 70s came from a phrase Evangelist Oral Roberts coined back in the 60s, "Christ in the now." Watching his program on Television and reading his books and materials had a profound effect on my life and ministry. Christ is in the now of our existence!

The Author

Contents

Forward

The messages you are about to read are not devotionals nor are they sermonettes. Although they were designed to be brief because of limited radio time, every message conveys a powerful, timely truth.

You will not journey far into the pages of this book before you realize that you are reading some of the most dynamic, anointed sermons ever delivered, either over radio, or from behind any pulpit in America. You are going to experience the heartbeat and evangelistic fervor of the author as each message challenges the unbeliever to receive Christ. You will witness a mixture of eloquence, humor, wisdom and urgency as the author, through these terse, concise messages, leads you on an exciting spiritual pilgrimage.

Let your heart sing as you are led into the glorious presence of the **Christ in the Now!**

Jerry C. Polk
Operations Manager
KMCT-TV39

1 — You've Got Questions? He's Got Answers!

There are many questions that plague the minds of people today. Such questions as: "Where am I going?" "What lies ahead for me?" "What about life after death?" "Will I go to Heaven?" "Will I go to Hell?" And, "Can I be sure about life?"

In order to have the abundant life that Christ offers, one must find the right answers to these and many other questions. These answers are found in Jesus Christ. He is God's gift to you because God sent Him to this earth to die and to make the way out of sin, the way past death and into Heaven. He arose from the dead and demonstrated He alone knew the way to eternal life. In fact, He stated, "I am the way, the truth and the life: No man cometh unto the Father but by me." Along life's path God has placed many signposts to point you to the abundant life He provides in Christ. Perhaps it has been a word of Scripture, a Christian's witness, a significant personal event, or it could be this radio program you're listening to today.

These signposts have been sent your way because God wants to lead you to the abundant life and salvation He offers today.

There are some that reason "all religions lead to Heaven." But God's word affirms, "There is none other name under Heaven given among men, whereby we must be saved." Jesus said, "I am the door" and He pleads with you to accept Him and follow His way. In fact, He stands at your heart's door right now and invites you to follow His way. His invitation is, "Come unto me, all ye that labour and are heavy laden, and I will give you rest."

You might question what does this abundant life include? According to the Bible it includes: joy, peace, love, guidance, rest, truth and knowledge, as well as power over sin, and hope that serves as an anchor for the soul. And today Jesus Christ wants to give these abundant life features to you. Today is decision day. Jesus is the only Savior. To reject Him now is to remain condemned. But to accept Him now is to find God's way to Heaven. This very moment you can be sure of salvation for the Scriptures state, "Believe on the Lord Jesus Christ, and thou shalt be saved. If we confess our sins, He is faithful and just to forgive us our sins."

Ladies and gentlemen, God wants to save you today. Therefore, I admonish you to accept Jesus Christ in faith and prayer. He stands at the very door of your heart and says, "If any man hear my voice, and open the door, I will come in to him and will sup with him and he with Me." Why not let Him now?

Let us pray. Almighty God, I pray for those of this radio audience who are unsaved. May they find abundant life in Christ. In Thy name I pray. Amen.

2 — Grace for an Inmate

A few weeks ago I received a letter, which stated, "Dear Rev. Reed: I am an inmate at the state reformatory. I'm writing this because I want to find peace with God. I really don't know the man you call God but I have heard lots about Him and His wonderful power. I'm a drug addict, and I want to be able to kick my habit through God's power."

I answered this young man in these words, "Received your letter inquiring about how you could find God. I was so happy to read this letter because it always causes me to rejoice when I meet or hear from people who want to find the God that has meant so much to my life."

Then in my letter to this young inmate I outlined four steps for Him to follow in finding peace with God. These four steps I would like to outline for you on this "Christ in the

Now" broadcast. First, acknowledge that you are a sinner. Romans 3:23 states, "All have sinned and come short of the glory of God." Ladies and gentlemen, you are not alone in this. Every person you know and are associated with comes under the fact of sin.

Second, recognize the end result of sin. Romans 6:23 says, "For the wages of sin is death." When we work we expect wages for what we do. The Scriptures teach that the same is true in sin: it demands wages for the wrongs done.

Third, realize that Jesus Christ can save. Again, we refer to Romans 6:23. The latter part of the verse says, "The gift of God is eternal life through Jesus Christ our Lord." Christ alone can save your life, for the Scriptures teach that "neither is there salvation in any other: for there is none other name under Heaven, given among men, whereby we must be saved."

The fourth step in finding peace with God is to receive Jesus Christ into your heart. John 1:12 says, "But as many as received Him, to them gave He power to become the sons of God, even to them that believe on His name." If you will open your heart and life to Christ He will come in.

In my letter to this inmate at the state reformatory I asked him to pray this prayer: "Dear Lord Jesus, I come before Thee with all sincerity of heart. I acknowledge that I am a sinner and I also recognize the end result of sin and where I will spend eternity without God. I believe on the Lord Jesus Christ and confess with my mouth my faith in Him. I realize that only Christ can save and I come to you in faith believing. I repent of my sins and invite Jesus Christ into my heart. Oh God, come into my heart, right now, I pray in the name of Christ. Amen."

And now the beautiful part of this story comes in a letter received from this prison inmate this past week. He said, "I know Jesus Christ came into my life in answer to that prayer you sent me. I simply accepted God at His word. Because God can't lie, Jesus Christ actually took up residence in my life and began to live in me, and He's been living there ever since. I bowed my head and simply prayed, 'God, I don't understand all of this. I don't understand how you're going to change my life. I don't even understand why I'm praying to you, but if these things are true, if what this preacher says is true, if you can transform my life and make me a new person, if you can forgive me of every sin that I have ever committed, then I'm asking you to do it. I'm asking you to come into my life and take it over and live in me.'"

Then he wrote, "There were no trumpets, no shouts, no vision. But He did just that. I know Jesus Christ came into my life in answer to that prayer. I know that the Christ I've committed myself to isn't just some fictitious character who lived two thousand years ago, some nebulous spirit floating around in the air somewhere. I know that Jesus Christ is alive and He's real!" Then, he closed his letter by saying, "This type of life can only be purchased by the person of Jesus Christ."

Ladies and gentlemen, what Christ did for this prison inmate, He can do for you. This is something that has happened in the last few weeks. And what God did for him, He is willing to do for you. I ask you right now to simply follow these four steps:

1. Acknowledge that you are a sinner.
2. Recognize the end result of sin.
3. Realize that Jesus Christ can save.
4. Receive Jesus Christ into your heart.

Pray with me right now that Christ will come into your life and set you free from sin.

Almighty God, we come into Thy presence on behalf of those of this radio audience that are not saved. I pray that this very moment as they acknowledge that you alone can save and meet the need of their lives that they will feel the wonderful presence of Jesus Christ. May they know the joy of being born again. In Thy name I pray. Amen!

3 — The Man Who Asked for Alms and Got Legs!

In the book of Acts, chapter 3, we have recorded the first apostolic miracle. As Peter and John went up together into the temple at the hour of prayer they met a man who had been lame all of his life. Each day he would be taken to the gate of the temple to ask alms of them that passed by. On this occasion, he saw Peter and John and looked to them for alms. Peter looking down at the man said, "Silver and gold have I none; but such as I have give I thee: In the name of Jesus Christ of Nazareth rise up and walk." And the lame was made whole by the power of Jesus Christ.

When this miracle occurred many people came to Peter and asked by what power or authority he did this. Peter told them that it was through the name of Jesus that he was healed. As a result of this miracle and Peter's discourse, many people who had heard the word and had seen the miracle began to believe on Jesus Christ. Before Jesus returned to Heaven He delegated this healing ministry to His disciples. He commissioned them to go out into all the world with a twofold message: to preach the forgiveness of sins and the healing of the sick. He said: "Go ye into all the world, and preach the gospel to every creature. He that believeth and is baptized shall be saved; But he that believeth not shall be damned. And these signs shall follow them that believe; in my name shall they cast out devils; they shall speak with new tongues; they shall take up serpents; and if they drink any deadly thing, it shall not hurt them; they shall lay hands on the sick, and they shall recover."

Sometimes the sick were healed individually, sometimes in masses. On at least one occasion God did special miracles so cloths coming from the body of the apostles were enough to transmit healing to the people. On another occasion the power of God was present to such an extent that even the shadow of an apostle falling upon the diseased was enough to bring healing to them.

As we look into the Scriptures we conclude that the duty of the Church in this matter is clear. The Church is called to preach and practice divine healing and when believers are sick, their first resort is to pray. For the Bible says, "Is any among you afflicted? Let him pray." It further says, "Is any sick among you? Let him call for the elders of the church; and let them pray over him, anointing him with oil in the name of the Lord: and the prayer of faith shall save the sick, and the Lord shall raise him up." The Old Testament prophet said, "With His stripes we are healed" and the New Testament apostle declared, "Christ...His own self bare our sins in His own body on the tree, that we, being dead to sins, should live unto righteousness: by whose stripes ye were healed."

The question is asked today, "Can we expect miracles in the 20th century?" Ladies and gentlemen, I find no place in the Scriptures that God's miracle working power is any less potent today than it ever was. God's power has been manifested in every age and the Scripture states that Jesus Christ is the same yesterday, today, and forever.

Our Heavenly Father wishes to reveal to us His love and to manifest the power of Christ. He desires for us to exercise our faith, and to confirm it, and to make us prove the power of redemption in the body as well as in the soul. Wherever the Spirit acts with power, there He works divine healings. Therefore, let us pray earnestly for the Holy Spirit. Let us place ourselves unreservedly under His direction and let us seek to be firm in our faith in the name of Jesus, whether for salvation or for the manifestation of His power in healing. Every blessing we have for both soul and body, for mind and Spirit, comes to us through our Lord's death on the cross. It was God's way and He sent His son Jesus Christ to bear our sins and the bruising of His body was for the healing of ours. There is nothing mystical about divine healing. It is the gift of God, like salvation, and we appropriate it through simple faith. I believe that what God has said He will do. I urge you to believe it and healing will come.

Let us pray. Almighty God, the one who declared, 'I am the Lord Thy God that healeth thee.' I pray for those of this audience who need Thy touch today. At this moment may they feel the wonderful healing power of Christ flow through their bodies. Make them whole by Thy great and wonderful power. In Thy name I pray. Amen.

4 — The Strongest Arm of the Church

I believe that Sunday school is everybody's business. The late Mr. J. Edgar Hoover made a statement some years ago that nearly every Sunday school leader has repeated at some time or other. He said, "Boys brought up in Sunday school are seldom brought up in court." Later, he made another very potent remark when he said, "The electric chair is not the answer to crime deterrent, but the high chair."

The two most potential forces for good in America and the world are the Church and the home. In some ways, the greater emphasis can be placed on the home. God built the home at least four thousand years before He began the building of His Church. And the devil knows if he can destroy the home, he will have destroyed the Church. Therefore, it goes without saying that it is essential that the home and the Church labor together for the salvation of the whole man, the whole family, the whole community and the whole world. The Sunday school is often called an arm of the Church. In fact, I believe it is its strongest arm. It is the one place where each member of the family can gather with others of the same age and study God's word in an informal manner. It also affords a measure of social activity and fellowship that is needful for total mental and spiritual growth. The greatest influence for good in a child's life often has been his teacher. That influence lives on in later years and plays a great part in the molding of good character and the making of a solid citizen.

Ladies and gentlemen let me ask, are you a regular attendant in Sunday school? Or are you one of the 80% of Americans who will not be in God's house this morning? As pastor of the First Assembly of God Church in Great Bend, I would like to encourage you to be in Sunday school somewhere this morning. If you do not regularly attend Sunday school and Church, join us at the First Assembly of God.

5 — Glorified Guilt

On this Father's Day, I wish to mention three things that every father should be guilty of.

First, he should be guilty of being a Christian. The Bible tells us in I Timothy 2:4 that God wishes "all men to be saved, and to come to the knowledge of the truth." A Christian is a follower of Jesus Christ and there is nothing unmanly about following Christ. Jesus Christ was the greatest man to walk on this earth. Being a Christian is not just for womenfolk and children. God wants to save men just as much as anybody else. And fathers should give serious consideration to giving their hearts and lives to Jesus Christ.

Secondly, every father should be guilty of dedicating himself to God. The Bibles exhorts, "I beseech you therefore, brethren, by the mercies of God, that ye present your bodies a living sacrifice, holy, acceptable unto God, which is your reasonable service. And be not conformed to this world: but be ye transformed by the renewing of your mind, that ye may prove what is that good, and acceptable, and perfect will of God." A man who starts a family contracts for responsibilities that are God assigned.

A father, more than anyone else, is responsible for the spiritual life of the home. According to Scripture God holds a father responsible for the moral pattern of the home. The Bible warns that God is a "jealous God, visiting the iniquity of the fathers upon the children unto the third and fourth generation."

I believe that if a father will dedicate himself to God, he will have divine sanctions to back his purposes in life. God designed the home. His laws protect it. God placed man at the head of the home, and He intends for a man to act in that capacity. I wonder what the judgment day will decree upon the slipshod, happy-go-lucky attitudes of so many fathers who casually roll off the responsibility of moral and Christian responsibility upon their wives? This is not God's way. He wants the father to lead in this responsibility.

Third, every father should be guilty of making investments in the home. What investments are you making in your home besides furniture and groceries? Solomon looked back over his own childhood and said, "Hear ye children, the instruction of a father, and attend to know understanding. For I give you good doctrine, forsake ye not my law. For I was my father's son, tender and only beloved in the sight of my mother. He (my father) taught me also, and said unto me, 'Let thine heart retain my words: keep my commandments, and live.'"

Can it be said of you as God said of Abraham, "I know him that he will command his children and his household after him, and they shall keep the way of the Lord." A father rules by saying, "Do as I do" and not by "Do as I say."

The Bible says, "But if any provide not for his own, and specially those of his own house, he hath denied the faith and is worse than an infidel." This not only includes food, clothing, transportation, education, and vacation; but it means love, time, Sunday school and church attendance as well as discipline and companionship.

No greater honor is given to any man than to lead his entire family into the kingdom of God. I believe that a father can have a ministry that is as far-reaching as the greatest evangelist in our day. I challenge every father listening to this broadcast to take your family by the hand and lead them to Christ. As a result, you will be blessed and you will reap rich dividends.

Let us pray. Almighty God, I pray for every father listening to this program today. May they know the blessedness of a personal experience with Jesus Christ. And may they also know the wonderful thrill of leading their families in the ways of the Lord. In Thy name I pray. Amen!

6 — Ready for the Rascal

In the 16th chapter of Matthew we have recorded the Sadducees and Pharisees asking Christ for a sign from Heaven in relation to the times. The Lord responded by saying, "I see that you are very clever at prognosticating the weather, but you have no Spiritual understanding of the signs of the times." They could read the signs of a storm on the western horizon but could not understand the fulfillment of prophecy, which are the signs of the times. Most of us have experienced nature's storms, but according to Scripture the world is facing storms mightier than any physical wind or rain. It is facing Armageddon, pushed there by the irresistible forces of the antichrist. The storm clouds around us reveal that the great tribulation is fast approaching. On today's "Christ in the Now" broadcast, I would like to give you seven reasons how we can know the world is getting ready to receive the antichrist.

The first reason is world language. The antichrist will need a unity of speech to rule the earth. It is amazing that at this moment world commerce is done in the English language. If a person understands English he can do business in every nation on the face of the earth. The antichrist will need such a vehicle to ride to world supremacy and the English language stands ready for such use at this moment. One language is a potent force for unifying a world under supreme dictatorship.

The second reason the world is ready for the antichrist is the world transportation we have. Almost every year our world shrinks smaller because of jet transportation and satellite communications. The entire world watched President Nixon at the very moment he was eating or talking in China and Russia. Travel is no longer difficult as almost any part of the earth is within a few hours ride. And this will make it very convenient for the antichrist to have instant movement around the world.

Thirdly, world finance unified by one currency makes a convenient vehicle for the antichrist. The financial structure of our modern world is bound together by a World Bank and by United Nations financial missions.

The fourth reason for the world's readiness for the antichrist is world entertainment. It might be interesting to know that you can get the same type of entertainment in most of the capital cities on this earth, as you get here in the United States. Throughout the world the same kind of night clubs, dances and music are popular. Yes, entertainment is certainly a strong factor for unifying mankind into a one-world federation under the antichrist.

Fifth is world religion. The Council of Churches is working incessantly to create a world religion. I feel that the antichrist must have this in order to rule as he wishes. In Revelation 16:13, the Bible calls the man who assists the antichrist the false prophet and he will do miracles before the people. False religion is now growing like a prairie fire and it is a prophetic sign of the emerging of the antichrist.

The sixth reason the world is ready for the antichrist is the United Nations. In a most remarkable manner the instrument of the United Nations has brought the world together. It has become a sounding board for every conceivable human problem. It is an amazing instrument of unity, especially in the area of human need. And it could be just such an instrument that the antichrist will use to dominate the world.

The last reason the world is ready for the antichrist is the moral bankruptcy that exists in the world. Possibly there was never a time in history when there hasn't been a single nation that could stand up and guide the world in decent morals. From others we hear that some communist nations demand better morals of their people than so-called Christian nations. And this should stir the heart of every Christian.

Ladies and gentlemen, these are suggestive reasons why our world is now ready to accept the antichrist. This means that Christ's return is imminent. Therefore, we should be ready at all times for the coming of Christ. Are you ready should He come today? I am going to pray for you and I ask that you bow in the eternal presence of Christ as I pray.

Almighty God, I pray for those of this audience who may not be ready for the soon coming of Thy son. May they know the joys of salvation in this hour. In Thy name I pray. Amen!

7 — Resurrection Realities

Talleyrand, who held various positions under King Louis the 18th, Napoleon Bonaparte and Louis Phillippe, once asked one of the kings of France how he might start a great new religion like Christianity. The king observed that the answer was simple. He had only to be crucified and then rise from the dead on the third day. In this response the king reminded the former priest of the great distinctiveness of Christianity. Other religions of this world have had good teachings. Some have even produced martyrs. But only Christianity tells of the great Redeemer who died and rose again.

The apostles recognized the tremendous significance of the Resurrection and made it a prominent feature of their preaching. Even after being threatened with bodily harm they continued preaching this distinctive of their faith. For it is recorded in Acts 4:33 that "with great power gave the apostles witness of the resurrection of the Lord Jesus."

In this message today I want to bring to your attention three things that the resurrection proves according to the preaching and teaching of the apostles.

First, it proves the deity of Christ. When the Scribes and Pharisees asked Jesus for a sign proving His right to teach as He did, Jesus referred to His coming resurrection by saying, "There shall no sign be given to this generation but the sign of the prophet Jonah: For as Jonah was three days and three nights in the whale's belly; so shall the Son of Man be three days and three nights in the heart of the earth." When He was asked for a sign proving His authority to drive moneychangers from the temple, He again alluded to His resurrection by saying, "Destroy this temple, and in three days I will raise it up."

In this day when there is so much liberal theological influence in the world there is again a great need for emphasis on the supernatural and we can be sure nothing will do more to convince men of the deity of Christ than the declaration of His resurrection.

Secondly, the truth of the resurrection is also proof of the adequacy of Christ's sacrifice for the sins of the world. Paul said that Christ "was delivered for our offences, and was raised again for our justification." Had Jesus remained in the clutches of death, it would have indicated He died for personal guilt rather than for the sins of the world. But because of the complete adequacy of the atonement effected at Calvary, Christ was raised from the dead.

Thirdly, the resurrection of Christ is proof of the believer's resurrection. Men in every generation have been perplexed by the mystery of physical death, and they often look upon it with dread. But the truth of Christ's resurrection reminds people that the believer's resurrection is guaranteed. To the troubled saints in Thessalonica, Paul wrote, "For if we believe that Jesus died and rose again, even so them also which sleep in Jesus will God bring with Him." To the Corinthians, Paul was able to say, "Knowing that he which raised up the Lord Jesus shall raise up us also by Jesus."

Ladies and gentlemen, if we are true to the Lord, one day we shall hear the blast of the trumpet of God and we shall be caught up to be with the Lord.

At this Easter season it would be well for everyone to join the first visitors at the open tomb and hear the angel say, "Fear not ye...He is risen, as He said." He is alive today.

Does He live in your heart? If not, bow in His eternal presence as we pray.

Almighty God, we thank Thee for the hope of the resurrection. We pray that you would place this hope in every heart today. In Thy name I pray. Amen.

8 — A Rainbow for Every Cloud

Scientists tell us that when the speeding sunlight hits the giant prism of cloud, a multicolored rainbow shines. And when a rainbow appears, it reminds us of the promise of God to Noah after the great flood that covered the whole earth. It is recorded in Genesis 9 that God said to Noah and his sons, "I establish my covenant with you and your descendants after you. I establish my covenant with you, that never again shall all flesh be cut off by the waters of a flood, and never again shall there be a flood to destroy the earth. This is the sign of the covenant which I make between me and you and every living creature that is with you, for all future generations: I set my bow in the cloud, and it shall be a sign of the covenant between me and the earth. When I bring clouds over the earth and the bow is seen in the clouds, I will remember my covenant which is between me and you and every living creature of all flesh."

To Noah and his descendants, the rainbow has served as the brightest symbol of hope, not only for their security, but also for their access to a just, holy and loving God. No doubt, Noah encountered many problems that are similar to what people have today. For along life's highway, we are aware that we shall encounter problems. We discover that young and old alike, the educated and the uneducated are not exempt from the problems of life. Life is a mixture of joy and sorrow, of successes and failures.

In the Old Testament times, there was a man whose name was Job. He feared God and abhorred evil. In the land of Uz, he was the richest man. But God allowed Satan to strip him of his wealth, in order to test his faith. Calamities befell Job. His oxen, asses, and camels were stolen, his sheep and servants were killed by fire, and his children died when a violent wind wrecked the house in which they were eating. Job himself, got boils all over his body and he sat and groaned in ashes. It was indeed a very painful experience. It was true at times he was discouraged, but his faith in God remained anchored despite his terrible sufferings. And in the end, the Lord blessed faithful Job more than his previous prosperity.

The Apostle Paul said that the sufferings of this present time are not worthy to be compared with the glory that shall be revealed in us. "For our light affliction, which is but for a moment, worketh for us a far more exceeding and eternal weight of glory."

Ladies and gentlemen, the days may be cloudy and stormy for you, but remember there is a rainbow for every cloud, and the rainbow is a sign of God's promise. If you will remain steadfast and anchored in Christ you will come through your storm victorious. David said, "The Lord is my Shepherd, I shall not want." Job said. "I know that my Redeemer liveth." Jesus said, "I will never leave thee nor forsake thee but I will be with you always even to the end of the world." Paul said, "I know whom I have believed and am persuaded that he is able to keep that which I have committed unto him against that day."

There is a promise in the Word of God for every need of your life–the rainbow for every cloud assures you of God's presence. I ask of you, right now, to bow in the eternal presence of the Son of God and appropriate His promises to your life and you can know the assurance of His presence.

Let us pray. Almighty God we bow in Thy presence on behalf of each one listening to this broadcast. You know their need; you know the cloud that surrounds their lives. I pray that the assurance of your presence shall grip their lives. In your name I pray. Amen.

9 — Broken Cisterns and Empty Lives

It is recorded in Jeremiah 2:13 that God said, "My people have committed two evils; they have forsaken my fountain of living waters, and hewed them out cisterns, broken cisterns, that can hold no water."

The background of this indictment is the fact that the nation of Israel had left the worship of the God who had brought them out of Egypt. They forsook the one who had given them a land that flowed with milk and honey, and had subdued the inhabitants before them. They had turned to the defiled worship of their neighbors that had led to judgment. The prophet laments that the people had exchanged their glory for that which would not profit. It is rather obvious that in our world, nation, communities, and even in our churches there is a situation resembling the state of Israel in the days of Jeremiah. There is the constant temptation to turn after the idols of the world. I know that we do not literally bow before wood and stone as they did, yet, we give our attention and our affections far too much to various things that dim our vision of the one true God.

The first tragedy the prophet sees is forsaking God. This is an act of gross ingratitude and forgetfulness for the multitude of blessings He has bestowed on us. God said, "Ye have forsaken me, the fountain of living water." In the Scriptures water is used as a symbol of life, and God is the fountain of living water. In forsaking God we have forsaken the source of our life, strength, and our joy. It is indeed a great evil for those who have once shared in the life of Christ and have partaken of the Heavenly blessings of God to seek elsewhere for fulfillment of life.

The second evil is the result of the first. Having left the fountain of living waters, people always try to fill the vacancy left in their lives in some other way. For some reason we are loath to come back like the prodigal son and confess that we have missed the mark. We would rather labor with a pick and shovel to dig our own cisterns than to return to the fountain where we can drink freely without labor. The tragedy is that the cisterns we dig to replace the fountain of life always develop leaks. My friends, there is no substitute for fellowship with God. There is no other restoration for the souls of men. In vain do we try to find the joy and richness of life that can renew the soul from our cracked and broken cisterns.

There are four broken cisterns that men and women today are digging out in their efforts to replace the reality of a vital experience with God. The first of these is material possession. Many hope to fill the void in their lives by accumulating wealth, conveniences, and possessions that add to their prestige. This is a great temptation because of the affluence of our society, but it is evident that these things do not really satisfy because Jesus said, "A man's life consists not in the abundance of things he possesses." The second broken cistern is the pleasures of the world. We live in a day when abundance of pleasures is available and attractive. Millions are spent advertising the pleasures man can engage in to satisfy the longing of his soul. Yet, in the end there is despair because pleasure is only a fleeting thing. The Bible teaches that "he that lives in pleasure is dead while he lives."

Another broken cistern is the pursuit of human philosophy. No matter how much man may think about the meaning of life, no matter how much he may learn about the world we live in, he cannot come up with the ultimate answers. The mind of man is degraded because the Bible says, "The natural man receiveth not the things of the Spirit, for they are foolishness to him." The only fountain of living water that will satisfy the mind and soul of man is a revelation of God through His word.

And finally, others have turned to a form of godliness. Our churches today are filled with people who have substituted the forms of religion for a real experience with God. In doing this they have dug themselves a broken cistern; they have missed the real water of life. Formal religion without the vitality of the fullness of God and the manifestation of His Spirit is only an empty shell. It is a form of godliness, but denies the power of it and it is therefore a broken cistern. On the other hand, there is a fountain of living water that flows freely and that is God. This fountain flowed through the life of our Lord Jesus Christ when He walked on the earth. Jesus said, "He that believeth on me, out of his innermost being shall flow rivers of living waters."

It is the will and purpose of God that every believer is an extension of this source of life that comes from God himself. Therefore, every child of God listening to this program should ask himself if his life is a channel for the fountain of living waters which the world is invited to come to and live. Let us not hew out broken cisterns, but let us return to the true and everlasting fountain.

Let us pray. Almighty God, forgive us of our sin of forsaking you and seeking satisfaction of life apart from the life giving water that you provide. Help us to return to you that this water can flow freely into and through our lives. I pray in Thy name. Amen.

10 — The Only Sin God Refuses to Forgive

Have you ever noticed that when people curse and swear they will use the name of God and of Christ, but we never hear any one swear by the name of the Holy Spirit? The reason for this is that something puts a check on them before they blaspheme and take the name of the Holy Spirit in vain. Jesus said, "Blasphemy against the Holy Ghost shall not be forgiven unto men." It is bad enough to commit sins that can be forgiven, without going so far as to commit a sin that Jesus said would never be forgiven.

I want us to take note of the possibility of sinning against the Holy Spirit by deeds and action. When you hear a gospel message and you feel something urging you to accept and believe, it is the work of the Holy Spirit. And when you reject salvation you are not rejecting the preacher but the Spirit of God. The Bible says that no one can come to God except the Spirit draw him. Therefore, you should be careful not to reject because the Bible says the "Spirit shall not always strive with man." If the Spirit of God ever ceases to strive with you, you will be lost eternally.

King Saul of the Old Testament came to this place when he continually rejected the ways of the Lord. The prophet came to him and said, "Because thou hast rejected the word of the Lord, he hath also rejected thee." When the Holy Spirit strives with you, you are never the same again. If you yield and accept you will be saved, but if you reject, your heart will be harder than ever. If, when God calls and you reject Him, there may come a day when He will not hear. It is recorded in Zechariah 7:13, "Therefore, it is come to pass, that as he cried, and they would not hear; so they cried, and I would not hear, saith the Lord of Hosts." The Apostle Paul tells us not to "Grieve the Holy Spirit of God." Again the Apostle says, "No man can say that Jesus is Lord, but by the Holy Ghost." If you are without Christ you cannot possibly be saved too soon, but there is the possibility you might wait too long and be lost eternally.

Men have been known to lose their health and to regain it. They have been known to lose friends and to win back lost friendships. However, when a soul is lost it is lost for eternity. Therefore, the matter of the Holy Spirit dealing with your life is of utmost importance. You cannot be saved without the help of the Holy Spirit. This is why I ask you in this hour not to resist but yield your life totally to Jesus Christ. During the next 20 seconds I want you to think seriously about eternity. I will be back to pray with you for your salvation.

As you feel the Spirit of God speaking to your heart don't turn Him away. The story is told of a certain minister who was called to the bedside of a dying woman. She said, "Dr. Guthrie, years ago I heard you preach. I was under conviction, but I said, 'Holy Spirit, leave me alone.' He did, as I have never been under conviction since. I do not have the feeling of conviction now, I am lost."

Ladies and gentlemen, don't resist the Holy Spirit, but yield right now as we pray.

Heavenly Father, we feel Thy Holy Spirit speaking to our hearts right now. I ask that You will come into the hearts of every one bowing in Thy presence right now. May they feel the warmth of the presence of God. May the joys of sins forgiven flood their souls. Give them the assurance of their salvation. In Thy name I pray. Amen.

11 — The Master's Reply to a Beggar's Cry

The poor beggar by the side of the road was by no means an unusual sight in the little country of Palestine. The entire nation had been reduced individually and collectively to poverty by the grinding hand of Roman imperialism. A person with even a minor mental or physical defect would find it impossible to keep pace with the hustle and bustle necessary to maintain even a starvation standard of living.

The Bible records a man sitting alone by the wayside. He was unattractive and unappealing to the casual eye. He wore tattered garments. He was the product of a people who for years had served God in form only and with outward display. When he heard the muffled tread of sandaled feet in the thick dust, the panting breath and chattering of the nearing mob, his remaining senses were alerted.

To him a crowd meant many things. Crowds meant people and it was upon people's generous giving that he depended for a livelihood. It must have been an unusual event. Even the blind beggar, as incapacitated as he was, could have detected if it was an oriental parade or a marriage procession with its gaiety and merriment.

But this event was no ordinary thing. The multitude arrived at the place where the man was sitting. The lazily lying dust of the twisting, parched pathway, disturbed by the intrusion of the many pairs of feet, rose in protest, invading his flared nostrils as if to warn him that this army of migrants might also tread on him. But the dust's warning was lost on him for his senses reached out past his own physical body to grasp the personality of the mob. Someone took time to tell the beggar that Jesus of Nazareth was passing by. His faith quickened and he cried out, "Thou son of David have mercy on me."

In that hour something takes place in his life, as he is set free by the mighty power of God. To the tortured bodies of today's narcotic addicts, there seems no peace. The inflamed stomachs of the alcoholics find no remedy. Life can be as futile and useless to them as to the blind beggar of the Jericho

Road. But ladies and gentlemen, lift up your heads, listen and learn. There is an attraction that is becoming central and it is Jesus the Son of God. When Jesus was upon this earth, he attracted lepers to himself as He walked in the wayside. He attracted angels to His side as He fasted in the wilderness. He attracted Satan, luring him into open combat, defeating him once and for all to smash his terrible power over mankind. At this moment poverty, sickness, and death stalk across our land bringing havoc, and leaving in its wake unbearable misery. But hard upon their heels, come mercy, hope, and love to bind up the broken hearted, to relieve the sting of death, to heal the fevered brow and to repair damaged lives.

The presence of Christ is with you right now and His voice from eternity is answering your cry of faith. His eye is upon you and His ear is open to your cry. His arms are outstretched to receive you now. He desires to hear your petition; therefore, I ask you to join with me in prayer right now.

Let us pray. Almighty God we bow in Thy eternal presence. I ask that your presence shall fill each heart and life listening to this broadcast. Meet every need of their lives right now. In Thy name I pray. Amen.

12 — Keen Teens?

Quite often in today's world we get a distorted picture of young people, the way they live and what they believe. Therefore, I would like to counteract this image that is so often projected through the news media and state my firm belief that I believe in young people. I believe that the right motivation and sense of direction can get the job done. They have energy, vitality, enthusiasm, inventiveness, creativity and stick-ability that only teenagers can have. As we look to the past we take note of the fact that men of mature years cannot claim to have made all the contributions to world progress. There have been teenaged inventors and scientists who have written headlines along the road to our more advanced civilization. Let us note some of these.

It was a seventeen year old Galileo who startled the scientific world with his treatise on the pendulum. It was a fifteen year old James Watts who became curious about the steaming teakettle in the kitchen. As a result of this curiosity he perfected the steam engine and became famous. It was Thomas Edison who took out a patent on an automatic telegraph repeater when he was seventeen. And it was fifteen-year-old George Westinghouse who designed the rotary engine while working in his father's machine shop in New York.

Ladies and gentlemen, this is just a small part of what teenagers have done in the past and I firmly believe that the same kind of ingenuity exists in the teens of today. There have also been teens that have contributed to the headlines on the world of religion. Billy Graham has asserted that teens are the "greatest evangelists in the world." This I believe, for once converted, the teens have tremendous potential as witnesses for Christ. There are three things I would like to challenge the teens of the "Christ in the Now" radio audience to do.

First, commit your life to Jesus Christ. Teens are developing, growing and changing. They want to become something they are not and this is provided for in Christ, for the Scriptures declare, "As many as received Christ, to them gave He power to become the Sons of God." Teens need Christ as Savior, Lord and Master of their lives.

Secondly, I would like to challenge you to demand respect in this world by the life you live. The Bible says, "Let no man despise thy youth, in conversation, in charity, in spirit, in faith and in purity." "Flee also youthful lusts...follow righteousness, faith, charity and peace."

Thirdly, I would like to challenge the teens of this radio audience to become involved in Christian services. I do not necessarily mean full-time Christian service, because I believe that with Christ every duty of life is religious. When we have separated the way of life into two parts and called one part secular and the other religious we have made a great mistake. For with Christ it was just as religious to heal a man as to offer a prayer or a burnt offering. Becoming involved in this kind of service and activity will mean helping your fellow man in any way possible.

With a life committed to Christ, living according to the Scriptures and engaging in Christian service, you will find the greatest fulfillment and happiness that anyone can find. I ask you to bow in the presence of Christ and accept these three challenges as we pray.

Almighty God, I come to you on behalf of the many teens of this audience, that are hearing me right now. Many of them are searching for truth. In their quest for life's meaning and purpose, may Thy Holy Spirit direct them to the Christ who can meet every need of their lives. In Thy name I pray. Amen.

13 — The King is Coming

Events of this past week have proven once again the validity of the Scriptures. It is recorded in the 24th chapter of the Gospel according to Matthew that the disciples of Christ came to him and asked, "What shall be the sign of Thy coming and of the end of the world." Jesus enumerated many things that would happen just prior to His return. He stated that one of the signs would be "earthquakes in diverse places." The earthquake in Southern California, as well as in other places around the world fulfills the prophecy of our Lord. Therefore, I feel it is imperative that we look into God's Word and once again examine the truth of the Second Coming of Christ.

First, let us take note of the certainty of His coming. The Bible teaches that He is coming again. We are told scores of times in the Scriptures that Christ will return. In fact, there are

318 references to the Second Coming of Christ in the New Testament. In the upper room as Christ talked to the sorrowing disciples, He told them that He was leaving them for a while, but that He would be coming back. It is recorded in John 14 that Jesus said, "Let not your heart be troubled: ye believe in God, believe also in me. In my Father's house are many mansions: if it were not so, I would have told you. And if I go and prepare a place for you, I will come again, and receive you unto myself; that where I am, there ye may be also." Ladies and gentlemen, I feel the Second Coming of Christ is the greatest certainty of the future.

The second truth we note concerning the Second Coming of Christ is the time of this event. The Bible teaches that no man knows the exact time of His coming. The time-setters are mistaken because we cannot tamper with God's timetable. Jesus said in Mark 13:32, "But of that day and that hour knoweth no man, no, not the angels which are in Heaven, neither the Son, but the Father." Even though we do not know the exact time of His coming the signs around us point towards this great day. Coming events have cast their shadows before, telling us that the Lord will soon be back. Jesus said in Matthew 24:6–7, "And ye shall hear of wars and rumors of wars: see that ye be not troubled; for all these things must come to pass, but the end is not yet. For nation shall rise against nation, and kingdom against kingdom; and there shall be famines, and pestilences, and earthquakes in diverse places."

The third thing we note in relation to this event is the results of the coming of Christ. And as we look into the word of God we find four groups to be dealt with at His coming.

1. The dead in Christ shall rise first as the bodies of all those who died trusting Jesus will wing their way upward to meet the Lord in the air.

2. The living Christians will be caught up to meet Christ in the air.
3. The lost dead will remain in their graves for a thousand years longer for it is recorded in Revelation 20:5, "...the rest of the dead lived not again until the thousand years were finished." Thus, the Bible teaches two resurrections from the dead: the resurrection of Christians when Jesus comes in the air, and the resurrection of the sinner, which shall happen a thousand years later.
4. The fourth group to be dealt with at the coming of Christ will be the sinners who are left on this earth to face the great tribulation.

I ask you this morning, are you ready should Jesus come today? Would you be caught up to meet the Lord in the air or would you be lost? Jesus stands ready to come into your heart right now, so that you can be ready for His coming.

14 — Provisions for Parenting

During the last several weeks I have counseled and prayed with a large number of teenagers who are beset with many difficult and perplexing problems. In trying to get to root of their problems, I have inquired concerning their family life and have found home life virtually nonexistent in many cases. I have found that many times children are taken for granted and often it is assumed that they are already adults. Many have gathered the impressions they are not wanted or needed. Many homes have suffered disintegration due to a lack of family loyalty or interest. As a result, we are reaping a generation of kids who have no real basis for life and many are turning to drugs and even to devil worship to find the answers they are searching for.

I feel it is time for moms and dads across America to wake up and take inventory of themselves, their homes, and their children. The relationship between the husband and the wife and the relationship of both to the children are exceedingly important. A sense of responsibility toward each other must prevail. I believe parents are to be examples.

We owe our children more than money. We owe them the finest manhood and womanhood in our redeemed nature. As parents, it becomes our task to make our homes so wonderful that the coming generation will treasure the inheritance of a happy, wholesome home life, filled with the sunshine of God's love. Homes do not just happen, they are the result of perpetual thought, discipline, prayer and action. Our homes should be more than just a house. And I feel we can safely conclude that the house is not a home until it is planted in Christ and when this happens it becomes the greatest institution on earth.

Since the success or failure of the home life depends primarily on the parent I would like to address myself to them for the next few minutes. I would like to present, from God's Word, duties and responsibilities of the parents.

First, you are to manifest love. To love and to be loved is one of the greatest riches in life for love is something you cannot give away and lose, but you always get more in return. In fact, love is essential to life. But in order to have the right kind of love we first must love God. The Bible asks, "If we love not our brethren whom we have seen, how can we love God whom we have not seen?" Ladies and gentlemen, without love the home cannot exist.

Secondly, you are to provide a home that is a shelter from the storms of life. The home should be a place where we can go when we want to shut out a world of strife. This should be our own small world of love, a place where the feeling of belonging and the togetherness helps us to know that we are a part of something wonderful.

The third duty and responsibility of the parent is found in Proverbs 22:6 that says, "Train up a child in the way he should go: and when he is old, he will not depart from it." Many consider teaching and training the same thing, but I feel a distinction can be made. To teach means to give instructions as how to do something, but to train means to demonstrate the instructions you have taught. We should not only give our children rules to live by, but we are to go further and train them by the rules found in God's Word. For once a child has been trained, he cannot be easily changed.

It is easier to take your children to church than to send them. It is easier to demonstrate love than to merely teach such. As parents, we are devoid of grace and wisdom to accomplish the great task that has been given to us. Therefore, we must look to God who has called us to be parents. It is in God alone that we can fit ourselves for the molding of souls. Even though children are a heritage of the Lord, yet, with that heritage we receive a commission to present our children again to Him.

As parents despairing of our own ability, let us go to God in faith so that we can do all things through Christ who strengthens us. Lacking in wisdom, let us "ask of God, that giveth to all men liberally, and upbraideth not; and it shall be given us." Failing in resource, let us seek Him who has promised to supply all our needs according to His riches in glory. Requiring faith, let us simply ask and we shall receive from the very Author of faith Himself.

Let us pray. Heavenly Father, I pray for every parent, every home in which this broadcast is heard. May the parents who now hear Thy Word, turn to you and seek your will and guidance for their lives. Help each one to recognize the tremendous responsibility that is theirs. As a family unit may each one who has heard this broadcast find their way to the house of God today so that their lives can be fortified through the power of God against the onslaught of evil. In Thy name, I pray. Amen.

15 — Power for the Hour

God intended that the gospel be preached and that it be preached everywhere. He has never required of man the performance of any task without first providing the ways and means for that task to be accomplished. And since we have been commissioned to spread the Gospel of Jesus Christ, He has given us the wonderful anointing of the Holy Spirit. To attempt to do the work of the Lord without this anointing would be a discouraging, difficult, and unsuccessful effort. The anointing of the Spirit was with the Son of God as He preached to the poor, as He healed the brokenhearted, as He preached deliverance to the captives, as He brought sight to the blind, as He set at liberty those who were bruised, and as He preached the acceptable year of the Lord.

This same anointing is also available to us today. Many tasks that confront the Christian are too difficult for him to do in his own strength and wisdom. Situations in which the Christian finds himself are often too complex for him to solve. The power of Satan that binds men and women is greater than human strength. God knew that these situations and many others like them would be encountered by His followers so to enable them to be equal to the task, He provided an anointing for service and that is what we call the anointing of the Holy Spirit.

The needs of humanity that were present in Christ's time are still prevalent today. There are still those people who are deprived and oppressed. He still appeals to the human heart, which cries out for help and understanding.

Human bondage, brought about by prison walls and chains, is a terrible plight but an even worse plight is the bondage of sin. What a joy and thrill it is to preach to the unsaved that through Christ, sin is pardoned, and that He no longer need be a captive to sin. Man's mere words cannot effectively convey the impact of this great message.

But man's words anointed by the Spirit, become powerful, penetrating and convincing.

Christ was also anointed to "set at liberty them that are bruised." That those who are chafed with the worries of life, those, who are perplexed with the problems of life, can find the liberating power of Christ real to their hearts and lives. The Bible says that "God anointed Jesus of Nazareth with the Holy Ghost and with power; who went about doing good, and healing all that were oppressed of the devil, for God was with Him."

I believe that in this 20th century we have every right to expect that signs will follow the preaching of God's word. We have a right to expect sinners to be delivered, believers to be filled with the Holy Spirit, the sick to be healed and demons to be cast out.

Let me ask, are you bound and unable to loose yourself from the bondage of this world? Do you long for the freedom of God's Holy Spirit in your life? Let me assure you that you can feel God's power right now, and you can know the fact of "Christ in The Now" is the need of your life. I'm going to pray for you and I ask you to pray. Open your heart to the heart of Jesus Christ. Reach out and touch Him right now and you can know the wonderful joys of freedom in the Lord.

Let us pray. Almighty God, I come to Thee on behalf of each one in this radio audience who is bound by Satan's power. May they experience the wonderful transforming power of Jesus Christ. Set the captive free. Let them know the power of Christ that is greater than any other power in this world. In Thy name I pray. Amen.

16 — Revival for Survival

The Bible says in II Chronicles 7:13–14, "If I command the locusts to devour the land, or if I send pestilence among my people: If my people which are called by my name, shall humble themselves and pray, and seek my face, and turn from their wicked ways: Then will I hear from Heaven, and will forgive their sin, and will heal their land."

I feel that the greatest need in the Church today is for the fires of evangelism to burn again. Thousands of souls are perishing. Degeneration and moral decay have gripped many. Coldness, lethargy, and lukewarmness are entertained in the hearts of those who should be burning with enthusiasm for Christ and His Church.

Revival is the answer here in America. I feel there are three things that should be done in the face of the Spirit that has gripped our land. First, there needs to be a burning compassion on the part of every professing Christian for the unsaved.

Many have fallen into a listless slumber, content to rest on their oars, while the lost perish. However, our responsibility is not fulfilled until every sinner is saved or crosses the dead line of God's grace and mercy in refusal and rejection of the message of salvation. In the past, some, from the nightmare of concentration camps, have cried out, "O, for another chance to prove my faithfulness to God and the Church." During World War II a minister of England said, "We were too busy to put God first. Now our time is taken up with war. We would not support the Church with our money. Now it is taken by the government to support the armed forces. We would not go to church when the bell rang. Now our church bells ring only when there is an air raid on." Ladies and gentlemen, I ask, "What will it take to stir our hearts to a return to God here in America?"

Secondly, there needs to be persistence in prayer on the part of the Christian. Philip Brooks said once, "As a painted fire is no fire and a dead man is no man, so a cold prayer is no prayer." In a painted fire there is no heat, in a dead man there is no life: so in a cold prayer there is no omnipotence, no devotion, and no blessing. Cold prayers are as arrows without heads, swords without edges, and birds without wings. They pierce not, they cut not, and they fly not up to Heaven. We need to shake ourselves away from cold praying and move into the warmth of the Holy Spirit, where we will be able to pray in an effectual and fervent manner for the souls of the lost.

Thirdly, there needs to be the straightforward preaching from our pulpits of the Word of God. Sermons should ring out like a fire alarm to awaken people out of their sleep. Like the sirens that send people running for the storm cellar or the bomb shelter, every sermon should send people fleeing for the ark of safety, which is Jesus Christ, the Lord. Sermons, that do not alarm the sinner and alert the Church, are dead.

When Peter preached at Pentecost, "They were pricked in their hearts." When Stephen preached they were cut to the heart. When John the Baptist preached, people from all walks of life said, "What shall we do?" The Philippian jailer cried, "What must I do to be saved?"

Ladies and Gentlemen, in America we need to return to God and Christians should take the lead by repenting and seeking God. We need to wake up and learn to appreciate our religious liberties before we lose them. We need to realize our obligation to the lost. For this day we need Jeremiah's tears, Joshua's courage, and the disciples' baptism of fire. We need to fall on our knees and cry out for His blessings to again rest upon our lives. Let us pray.

Almighty God, the Father of Jesus Christ and us all, we enter Thy presence asking that Thy Holy Spirit would grip our hearts with conviction. Help us to return to the old paths and seek Thy face in repentance. In Thy name I pray. Amen.

17 — Nothing but the Blood

There are many theories about eternal salvation. One of the most popular ideas is that a person can make up for his evil deeds by doing enough good ones. In other words, God won't let a few faults keep a person out of Heaven if he's a decent sort of fellow. God will simply put all of our deeds on His scales–the bad on one side, the good on the other–and if they come near to striking a balance we have no need to worry.

Then there is the slightly less popular theory of endeavoring to appease God by giving money to a church or a mission, or by building a temple. Giving money to God's work is a good deed and a commendable one, but eternal life is not for sale. Simon, the sorcerer, once offered Peter money and the Apostle said to him, "thy money perish with thee, because thou hast thought that the gift of God may be purchased with money."

A third theory concerning eternal salvation is the respectable and refined method of trust in one's character for salvation. That is, a person is born in a Christian country and imbibes Christian principles at home, at school and at church. He lives and works in a Christian environment, is bolstered by Christian influences on every hand, and adopts Christian standards and ideals. Therefore, he calls himself a Christian and thinks he is good enough to meet God's approval. But if such were the case, Christ never would have needed to die on the cross!

On the other hand, there are many like the jailer at Philippi who asked, "What must I do to be saved?" The answer from the Scriptures is very simple, very clear, and very definite, "Believe on the Lord Jesus Christ, and thou shalt be saved." Eternal life is a gift from God. No man can manufacture it and no man can earn it. It was purchased for us at Calvary when Jesus died for our sins, and we obtain it simply by repenting of our sins and trusting in His grace. A long time ago, on the night of the first Passover, the Israelites received a message from God. It told them exactly what to do in order to be saved. God told them to slay a Lamb and sprinkle the Lamb's blood on the doorposts of their houses. He said, "When I see the blood, I will pass over you." The New Testament says, "Without shedding of blood, is no remissions of sins." Therefore, we are not redeemed with our good works neither with silver or gold, but only "with the precious blood of Jesus Christ."

Ladies and gentlemen, I exhort you not to be fooled by any man's ideas, but rather, take God's way. Put your faith in the Lamb of God. Trust in the power of Christ's blood to cleanse you from all sin and to make you acceptable in the sight of God. Let us pray.

Almighty God, Giver of eternal life, I pray for those of this audience that are not saved. May they feel the wonderful flow of the precious blood of Christ upon their lives today. In Thy name I pray. Amen.

18 — Outer Space or Inner Peace?

People everywhere are concerned over what's happening in our world today. On the one hand we are astonished that our space team has been able to land on the moon's surface. On the other we are disturbed about the disorders in our cities, pollution, the awful poverty of millions in a land of plenty, the growing complexity of successfully pulling out our troops from bloody Vietnam, and the endless hassles in Washington over ways to get America out of this mess it's in. All these things are swirling around in people's heads today. On an individual basis people are concerned and distressed over rising prices, increased taxes, and the day-by-day struggles with their family, and their own soul needs. It's in the newspaper, it's in the speeches we hear from leaders, it's like rain falling day after day until the rivers and ponds are full and are now overflowing the fields and even coming into our homes. People sickened yet wake up each morning with more news of bad things happening in the world around them.

Yet there can be a calmness in the soul in spite of all the stress and misery and turmoil in our world today. The reason for this peace and calmness in the midst of the storm is that the believer is kept by the power of God and, as a result, has the feeling of peace, rest and joy within. No matter how dark things around you look, no matter how conditions try to envelop your life, your family, and everything you have and stand for, you can have a life in which God delivers you from this present world. You can be filled with every blessing of God, you can know God is going to take care of you, and you can have a witness for Him that no power on earth can stop.

To illustrate this truth, let me share with you a story I read the other day. A man riding a train suddenly felt the train lurch forward. The engineer had decided to make up lost time so he opened the throttle and poured on the power. When the train hit speeds of 100 and 110 miles per hour the passengers were thrown out of their seats. People were beside themselves with fear and cried out to one another for answers. All at once a little girl came running down the aisles, keeping upright by holding onto the edges of the seats nearest the aisle. After she had run through the entire train like this, a man frantically grabbed her and shouted, "Little girl! Don't you know there's something wrong on this train and we don't know what it is? How can you be so calm and run through the aisles as though you had no cares?" The little girl smiled and said, "Mister, my daddy is the engineer on this train and he knows I'm on it."

Ladies and gentlemen, this story serves to illustrate the authority of God's word. God is speeding up the time of the end. People everywhere are looking at the awful conditions around them and crying out in fear, as our God turns this special homeward it is His hand that is on the throttle. It is His timetable that He is going by, and He knows you and I are on board.

Therefore, I admonish you to stop worrying about wars and violence and man's failures to meet needs in your life and start looking up to God who has more resources that you can use in a lifetime. Stop being disturbed about the scientists going further into space. Just be sure you know the Holy One who made all space and who sent His blessed Son into your life with eternal and abundant life. Let us pray.

Almighty God, how great Thou art. How wonderful are Thy works and Thy ways are past finding out. I pray for those in this audience who are bound and tormented by fear as they look at the conditions that surround their life. Help them to know the calm and peace of the Holy Spirit in their hearts and lives. In Thy name I pray. Amen.

19 — What If…?

The late Robert Kennedy once said, "Some men see things as they are and say why. I dream things that never were and say why not?" I have often looked at things as they are and asked "What if..."

We know God as the self-existent and preexistent God. We are told He is the Light without any mixture of darkness and that He is love. What if (since He could be whatever He wanted to be) He had been all darkness without any mixture of light, and a God of vengeance instead of love? God created man in His own image and gave him the power of choice. What if man had been created as an automaton with no emotions and without the power to choose, to create, to love? What if...man, after rebelling, had been privileged to remain in the Garden with no restrictions to the Tree of Life, living forever in his sinful state? What if...Christ had not come and clothed Himself in human flesh that glorious night in Bethlehem? What if...He had not lived a sinless life and given to us a perfect example? What if...He had not gone all the way to Calvary and shed His blood "upon the altar to make an atonement for our souls?" What if... when His body was laid in the tomb, that had been the end? What if there was no resurrection? What if, when He left His disciples on Olivet, He did not get safely through the Heavens back to the right hand of the Majesty on High? What if...there were no hope of His Second Coming and our being gathered unto Him? What if...there was a hell but no Heaven, or a Heaven but no hell? What if there was no redemption at all?

The Apostle Paul expressed some "what ifs" in I Cor.15:12-19. He asked, "What if... there be no resurrection?" The results, Christ is not risen; our preaching is vain; your faith is vain; we are false witnesses; you are yet in your sins; they which are fallen asleep in Christ are perished; we are of all men most miserable. But Paul gives us the glorious alternative when he says, "But now IS Christ risen from the dead, and become the first-fruits of them that slept."

Many times I have heard people ask, "Why am I alive?" Answers to this question do not come easy, but allow me to pass on a few suggestions. What do you suppose God had in mind when He made us; and why has He kept us alive to this moment?

One reason surely is that He must have objects for His love. He could have directed His love into a vacuum but it would have brought Him little satisfaction. He evidently wanted people; men, women and children; as objects toward which He could lavish His love and on whom He could fasten His affections.

Also, God desires fellowship with persons who will choose to love Him. This puts Him in the position of being the recipient of something we produce. The Bible sets Him forth as a father who yearns to receive the loving attention of a wife. This adds a new dimension to my reason for existence. The Lord desires to receive love from a person such as me. Then, too, we are of value to Him as objects of His craftsmanship. Jeremiah likens God to a potter and us to clay. Ezekiel saw us as metallic ore. Isaiah sees us as bejeweled crowns and diadems to epitomize the beauty He sees in us that brings to Him pleasure and satisfaction. God loves you. Does that mean anything to you?

It is not within our providence to choose the circumstances of our birth, but we can choose where we will spend eternity and this is the biggest choice that life affords.

My friend, you can face these facts and realities of life if you have Christ in your heart. Why not let Him come in right now so that when the time of death, judgement and eternity comes to your life you will be prepared. Let us pray.

Heavenly Father, there are unprepared lives desiring to know Thee now. Let the Holy Spirit hover around each one who has heard this message and as they call on Thy name, bring peace and joy to their hearts. I pray in Thy name, Amen.

20 — Teen Power

At the First Assembly of God Church in Great Bend we are thankful for the wonderful group of teens the Lord has given us. I'm aware that many times we adults get a distorted image of teens but in this message I want to state my firm belief that I believe in young people and their ability to get the job done. Teens have energy, vitality, enthusiasm, inventiveness, creativity, and stick-ability that only teenagers can have.

As we look to the past we take note of the fact that men of mature years cannot claim to have made all the contributions to world progress. There have been teenaged inventors and scientists who have written headlines along the road to our more advanced civilization. I would like to note some of these.

It was seventeen year old Galileo who startled the scientific world with his treatise on the pendulum. It was fifteen year old James Watts who became curious about the steaming teakettle in the kitchen. As a result of this curiosity he perfected the steam engine and became famous. It was Thomas Edison who took out a patent on an automatic telegraph repeater when he was seventeen. And it was fifteen-year-old George Westinghouse who designed the rotary engine while working in his father's machine shop in New York.

Ladies and gentlemen, this is just a small part of what teenagers have done in the past, and I firmly believe that the same kind of ingenuity exists in the teens of today. There have also been teens that have contributed to the headlines in the world of religion. Billy Graham has asserted that teens are the "greatest evangelists in the world." This I believe, for once converted the teen has the tremendous potential as a witness for Christ.

On today's "Christ in the Now" broadcast I would like to challenge the teens of this audience to do three things. First, commit their lives to Jesus Christ. Teens are developing, growing and changing. They want to become something they are not. The Scriptures declare "That as many as received Him to them gave He power to become the sons of God."

Secondly, I would like to challenge the teens to demand respect in this world by the life they live. The Bible exhorts: "Let no man despise thy youth: but be thou an example of the believer's, in Word, in conversation, in charity, in spirit, in faith and in purity. Flee also youthful lusts...follow righteousness, faith, charity and peace." With a life like this respect is demanded.

Thirdly, I would like to challenge the teens of this audience to become involved in Christian service. I do not necessarily mean full-time Christian service, for I believe that with Christ every duty of life is religious. When we have separated the way of life into two parts and called one part secular and the other religious, we have made a great mistake. I believe with Christ it was just as religious to heal a man as to offer a prayer or a burnt offering. Becoming involved in this kind of service and activity will mean helping your fellow man in any way possible. With a life committed to Christ, living according to the Scriptures, and engaging in Christian service, you will find the greatest fulfillment and happiness that anyone can find. I ask you to bow in the presence of Christ and accept these three challenges as we pray.

Almighty God, I come to you on behalf of the many teens of this audience. Many are searching for truth and you are truth. In their quest for life's meaning and purpose, may the Holy Spirit direct them to the Christ who can meet every need of their lives. In Thy name I pray. Amen.

21 — God Wants You Full!

My emphasis on today's broadcast of "Christ in the Now" will be on the infilling of the Holy Spirit. Evangelist Billy Graham tells of preaching one Sunday morning in a certain church that had a problem. The problem was a deacon who came to church drunk. Dr. Graham stated that "The church had a congregational meeting and excommunicated him. This, they should have done." Billy Graham then turned to the pastor and said, "Does every deacon come every Sunday filled with the Holy Spirit?" The pastor answered, "No they don't!" Then, Dr. Graham said, "Did you ever kick them out for this offense?" And again, the pastor answered, "No." Billy Graham countered, "Why not? The same scripture that says, 'Be not drunk with wine,' also says, 'Be filled with the Spirit.'"

This story serves to illustrate the necessity of the infilling of the Holy Spirit. It is not a luxury, nor is it optional. Jesus commanded His disciples not to depart from Jerusalem until they had been filled with the Holy Spirit. The Apostle Paul used imperative language when he said in Ephesians 5:18, "To be filled with the Spirit." Therefore, we conclude from Scripture, that it is a command we must obey. To be filled with the Spirit is to experience that which the 120 disciples of the Lord experienced on the day of Pentecost when "They were all filled with the Holy Ghost and began to speak with other tongues as the Spirit gave them utterance."

This experience is often called the Baptism in the Spirit, because Jesus had described it in terms of a Baptism. John the Baptist even referred to it in these terms when he said, "I indeed baptize you with water unto repentance, but he that cometh after me is mightier than I, whose shoes I am not worthy to bear: He shall baptize you with the Holy Ghost, and with fire." Jesus mentioned it before he departed and ascended into Heaven by saying, "John truly baptized with water, but you shall be baptized with the Holy Ghost not many days hence."

This wonderful baptism is a gift from Heaven. The Bible describes this in Acts 2:1-4 in these words, "And suddenly there came a sound from Heaven as of a rushing mighty wind, and it filled all the house where they were sitting. And there appeared into them cloven tongues like as of fire, and it sat upon each of them. And they were all filled with the Holy Ghost and began to speak in other tongues as the Spirit gave them utterance." Jesus said, "He that believeth on me, as the scripture hath said, out of his belly shall flow rivers of living water. But this spake He of the Spirit, which they that believe on Him should receive: for the Holy Ghost was not yet given; because that Jesus was not yet glorified."

The striking point in this passage of scripture is the parallel that Jesus draws between the Holy Spirit and flowing rivers. To be filled with the Spirit is to have, "Rivers of Living Water" flowing from one's inmost being. What a tremendous ministry this opens up to everyone. Even those who may have considered themselves unimportant or with few talents, can do a significant work for God! The weakest and most obscure men and women can have this experience by believing on Jesus. Whatever your occupation, wherever you might be today, whether at home, in an office, at a factory, and regardless of your circumstances, if you will believe on Jesus you can receive the Holy Spirit and have "Rivers of Living Water" flowing from within. Let us pray!

Almighty God, giver and sustainer of life, we pray that Thy Holy Spirit would flow in hearts and lives right now. May those of this audience who are hungry for Thy blessed Holy Spirit be filled to overflowing right now. In Thy name I pray. Amen!

22 — Awaiting the Arrival

These are exciting days in which we live. The reason they are exciting is the blessed hope the Christian has of the coming of Christ. The Bible says, "This same Jesus shall come in like manner as ye have seen Him go into Heaven." That blessed hope calls for the reappearance of our Savior Jesus Christ. And we know that He is coming again because the Scriptures predict it. Many professors of religion have neglected the truth of His coming; some have even scoffed at this truth. Yet, Jesus is coming and it will be the very same Jesus who came the first time who will come again. As Christ ascended back to Heaven, after having come to this earth to give His life, the Heavenly messengers informed the little group of lowly disciples that "this same Jesus will come again." When He comes it will be with a variety of gestures. He will come as the high priest to bless His people, as the bridegroom to His church, as the Messiah to the Jews, as the reckoner for the servants, as the chief shepherd for the under shepherd and as the King of

Kings and Lord of Lords. When He comes, each of us will have to meet Him and it will depend on what we have done with His first coming as to how we shall be treated at His Second Coming.

First, I want you to notice that His Second Coming is SURE. Nothing can stop it. His first coming was divinely promised, gloriously and greatly accomplished. Similarly will His Second Coming take place, for Jesus has promised it, the angels have proclaimed it, the Scriptures have predicted it, and it is certain, nothing can stop it. Secondly, His coming will be SUPERNATURAL. The Bible teaches that He departed supernaturally for He "was taken up into Heaven in a cloud receiving Him out of their sight" and "He shall so come as ye have seen Him go." God will once more break into the affairs of this world in a supernatural way. Thirdly, His Second Coming will be SURPRISING. He is coming in such "an hour as ye think not," and more than a few will get the shock of their lives. Many will be surprised to hear His voice telling them to go away, that He doesn't know them and never did know them. Fourth, His Second Coming is going to be SUDDEN. Our Lord reminds us that it will be like the lightning that flashes. Paul informs us that it will all be over in the twinkling of an eye. No wonder Jesus urges us to, "be ye also ready for in such an hour as ye think not, the Son of man cometh." His coming will be SOON for Jesus said, "Behold, I come quickly and my reward is with me." The coming of our Lord draweth nigh for many of the signs and warnings given by the Holy Spirit through our Lord and the Apostles and prophets are taking place. And, as we see these signs being fulfilled, we cannot help but be excited at the approaching and intimate return of the bridegroom for the bride. Signs in the natural, educational, scientific, nuclear, moral, religious, military and Jewish realms all point to the soon return of Christ.

Are you ready for His return? If not, you can be ready. But you ask, "How can I be ready?" First, believe on the Lord Jesus Christ, secondly, confess with your mouth the Lord, and thirdly, let Christ come into your heart. For the Bible says, "...if thou shalt confess with thy mouth the Lord Jesus, and shalt believe in thine heart that God hath raised him from the dead, thou shalt be saved. For with the heart man believeth unto righteousness; and with the mouth confession is made unto salvation." "For as many as receiveth Him, to them gave He power to become the sons of God."

Let us pray. Almighty God, we enter into Thy presence with thankful hearts because of the hope of The coming we have. Yet, we realize there are those listening to us who are not ready. I pray that the Holy Spirit would speak to their hearts helping them in this moment of preparation for Thy coming. I pray in Thy name. Amen.

23 — The Christ for Every Crisis

A living Christ in a time of crisis is the message of this radio program. Contrary to what many think, God is alive today, doing His work of redemption, changing the lives of men and women, giving hope, health, and assurance in an age of anxiety. Our message presents a living God whose power has not been diminished with the passing of time. He is the God of Abraham, Isaac, and Jacob. He is the God who has revealed Himself through His Word, the Holy Bible, and who has spoken to us through His Son, Jesus Christ.

First, we present the Christ who saves. Hebrews 7:25 tells us that Christ saves you from the penalty of sin in hell. He can save you from your worries and fears. He can change your life and transform you from sinner to saint. He can give you a purpose for life and an inner strength to meet every problem.

Second, we present a Christ who heals. Only He can see you as a total person, body, soul, and spirit. His compassion extends to your physical body, even as He is able to see the needs of your soul and spirit. The Bible says, "He is the same yesterday, today, and forever."

Third, we present a Christ who empowers for service. He has promised to fill you with His Holy Spirit. The Bible says, "Ye shall receive power after that the Holy Ghost is come upon you, and ye shall be witnesses unto me." The Holy Spirit will not only abide with you and instruct you but He will provide you power for bringing the lost to Christ so that your witness will not depend upon "lofty words of wisdom...but in demonstration of the Spirit and power."

Fourth, we present a Christ who is coming again. He will come to take those who have faith in Him, "and so shall we ever be with the Lord." But He will also come to judge. First of all, He will judge every believer. He will not judge to condemn them but rather their works so he can reward them for their faithfulness. Then, he will judge the world. On that day, everything that is hidden will be revealed, and sin will be unmasked for what it is. Hypocrites will have no place to hide. The tares will be separated from the wheat, the sheep from the goats. Wolves will be stripped of their sheep's clothing. But those who have cast their allegiance to Jesus Christ will have no fear on that last day of crisis. The Bible says, "...little children, abide in Him, so that when he appears we may have confidence and not shrink from Him in shame at His coming." Life has many crises, and only a complete confidence in Jesus Christ, the Son of God, will help you overcome every one of them.

It is our prayer as you listen to this broadcast that you will meet Christ. And, believing in Him, you will find the answer for the crisis you are now facing. Let us pray.

Almighty God, meet every need of each one listening to this program. Save the unsaved, heal the sick, empower the believer for service and place the hope of Thy coming in every heart. We pray in Thy name. Amen.

24 — What Only Christ Can Do

The Christian faith is not a theory or a speculation; it is a way of life. The Christian faith is not something upon which to reflect; it is something upon which to act. Jesus Christ does not ask for your interest, he asks for your life. Faith in Christ is not an intellectual assent to a series of theological propositions. It is not mental assent to a set of philosophical principles. Faith is response to a person. Faith is venture, obedience, commitment and decision. The decision to serve Christ is one that no one else can make for you. Your minister cannot make your decision. Your friends can't respond to God for you. Your parents cannot do it: only you can. It is a decision that permits no neutrality for Jesus said, "He that is not with me is against me." But before we can make a valid decision about Christ, we have to know the issues involved in the choice. What is it that Jesus Christ does for a man that no one else can do? What does he bring to a man that no one else can bring? What is the claim that Christ makes for Himself? What is the claim that the Christian Church has made for 2,000 years?

To answer these questions, I bring to your attention three things that Christ alone can do for you. First, only Christ can save you from your sins. It is impossible to understand the Bible and the Christian faith unless we realize that this was and is the center and heart of the ministry of Christ. This is why He came to earth. When I look at the cross, I see my sin exposed. When I go to Calvary and see Jesus dying, I know that the things that brought Him there are the very things that I recognize in myself. I see the compromise of Pilate, the pride of the Pharisees, the treachery of Judas, the cowardice of the disciples, the heedless indifference and the cruelty of the crowds. When I look at the cross I know that I am guilty. I know that I am condemned, I know that by rights I should be hanging there. But, thank God I am not there. Because in the mysterious, unsearchable, unfathomable love of God, Christ is there, "bearing shame and scoffing rude. In my place, condemned He stood sealed my pardon with His blood, Hallelujah, what a Savior."

Secondly, only Christ can give you eternal life. Paul said, "The wages of sin is death; but the gift of God is eternal life through Jesus Christ." There are two types of life. There is natural life, which we share with all created things, the life that follows our creation. That life will die. But there is another life, and the New Testament calls it eternal life. It is the life that Jesus Christ came to give to you and me. It is the life of God in the soul of man. Through faith in Christ we are born again into the family of God. We are translated from the kingdom of darkness into the kingdom of His Son. This new life in Christ is given to us now.

Thirdly, only Christ can assure you of a place in Heaven after death,. Death is the final blow to the pride of man. Our passage through this world is but a brief passage. I am certain there is not a single thinking person who has not asked the questions: What lies beyond the last twilight and the setting sun? Is there anything beyond this world? How can I know? My friends, there is only one who can tell you. This one came back from the dead, He arose victorious over the grave, and He broke the bonds and shackles of death and now lives forever. He is the Lord Jesus Christ, the Son of God. He is the one who says, "I am the resurrection and the life: he that believeth in me, though he were dead, yet shall he live:"

I ask you to think seriously today. Jesus Christ came to bring you freedom from sin. He came to bring life to men. He came to give you power, standing by you everyday and interceding for you. He came to bring us victory over death, giving us an inheritance incorruptible and undefiled. Freedom, life, power and victory are things you need. Only Christ can give them to you. He summons you to faith in Him, to surrender your life, mind, heart and will. I plead with you to come to Him. Commit yourself to Him in faith. He will receive you. He will make you a new creature, He will save you from your sins and bring you into the family of God.

Let us pray. Lord Jesus, receive those into Thy kingdom who bow in Thy presence right now. I pray in Thy name. Amen.

25 — The Suffering Christ

The Scriptures teach that "Christ is touched with the feelings of our infirmities." He knows every sorrow, pain and disappointment that pierces your heart today. The purpose of this message is to reveal the relevancy of Christ to your need, and to do this, I want to share an article that came across my desk this past week.

It seems "at the end of time, billions of people were scattered on a great plain before God's throne. Some of the groups near the front talked heatedly, not with cringing shame, but with belligerence. A joking brunette said, "How can God judge us? How can He know about suffering?" This she said as she jerked back a sleeve to reveal a tattooed number from a Nazi concentration camp. As she reflected she said, "we endured terror, beatings, torture and death!" In another group, a black man lowered his collar. "What about this?" he demanded, showing an ugly rope burn. Then he exclaimed, "I was lynched for no crime but for being black! We have suffocated in slave ships, been wrenched from loved ones and toiled until only death gave release."

Far out across the plain were hundreds of such groups. Each had a complaint against God for the evil and suffering He permitted in His world. How lucky God was to live in Heaven where all was sweetness and light, where there was no weeping, no fear, no hunger and no hatred. Thus they questioned, "What did God know about what man had been forced to endure in this world? After all, God leads a pretty sheltered life."

So each group sent out a leader, chosen because he had suffered the most. There was a Jew, a black, an untouchable from India, an illegitimate, a person from Hiroshima and one from a Siberian slave camp. In the center of the plain they consulted with each other. And at last they were ready to present their case. It was rather simple: Before God would be qualified to be their judge, He must endure what they had endured. Their decision was that God "should be sentenced to live on Earth–as a man!"

But because He was God, they set certain safeguards to be sure He could not use His divine powers to help himself. They decreed that He should be born a Jew. Let the legitimacy of His birth be doubted, so that none will know who is really His Father. Let Him champion a cause so just, but so radical that it brings down upon Him the hate, condemnation and eliminating efforts of every major traditional and established religious authority. Let Him try to describe what no man has ever seen, tasted, heard or smelled.. Let Him try to communicate God to men. Let Him be betrayed by His dearest friends. Let Him be indicted on false charges, tried before a prejudiced jury and convicted by a cowardly judge. Let Him see what it is to be terribly alone and completely abandoned by every living thing. And let Him be tortured and let Him die! Let Him die the most humiliating death, that with common thieves.

As each leader announced his portion of the sentence, loud murmurs of approval went up from the great throng of people. When the last had finished pronouncing sentence, there was a long silence. No one uttered another word. No one moved. For suddenly all knew...God had already served His sentence.

Ladies and gentlemen, Christ has suffered for the unjust. He knows your needs this very moment and is desirous to touch your heart. He is willing and able to run to your cry for help. I ask you to bow in His eternal presence, talk to Him as you would a friend and allow His wonderful presence to fill your life as I pray.

Almighty God, our hearts rejoice in the truth that thou didst love us enough to come to this earth and die for our sins. I pray that Thy Holy Spirit would fill each one listening to this prayer today. In Thy name I pray. Amen!

26 — Born to Die

Jesus Christ did not come to earth simply to be born here. He did not come just to teach a new way of life. Jesus came to die, and His greatest victory, His greatest triumph, was on the cross where He conquered sin, hell and the grave. I believe of all the men who marched across the stage of time, Jesus was best fitted to lead the masses. He had supernatural courage. He was a real man. He was a man's man. He was a leader of men and He was an action man. Christ fed the hungry multitudes supernaturally. He healed the sick, raised the dead and gave sight to the blind. As long as Jesus was riding triumphantly into Jerusalem with multitudes throwing their coats on the ground, waving palms and shouting, "Hosanna to Him who cometh in the name of the Lord," He was their great prophet. But when He turned to them and explained that He must go to Calvary and die, His followers melted away. We question: "Why did they reject Him? Why did they turn away?" The answer lies in the stigma of Calvary because the world did not like the idea of a cross. Ladies and gentlemen, to become a Christian does cost. You must "deny yourself, and take up your cross, and follow Jesus." What is Calvary's stigma and what does it cost?

First, the stigma of Calvary involves separation. Calvary is a place from which cowards hide and brave men dare to stand. Calvary is a place where the good stand on one side and the bad on the other. Sometimes you have to stand alone when following Christ. A boy may find himself alone in school; a man may find himself alone in business, standing alone for moral principles. Noah had to stand alone, as did Abraham, Joshua, Elijah and Daniel. Jesus said, "But whosoever shall deny me before men, Him will I also deny before my father which is in Heaven. Think not that I am come to send peace on earth: I came not to send peace, but a sword. For I came to set man at variance against his father, and the daughter against her mother, and the daughter-in-law against her mother-in-law. And a man's foes shall be they of his own household." Yes, we have to stand the stigma of separation sometimes for Christ.

Secondly, the stigma of Calvary involves desertion. When Christ was facing the cross He knew that He would have to suffer alone. He knew that even His best friends and followers would desert Him. He knew that those who cried, "Hosanna!" on Palm Sunday would cry, "Crucify, Crucify!" tomorrow. He knew that Judas would betray Him and Peter would deny Him. He knew the street crowds would turn on Him. Thus, He found the cross a very lonely place. Ladies and gentlemen, would you like to live close to the Christ crucified? Would you like to live close to the old rugged cross? Then, you're going to have to say, "Lord, I'll bear the shame." In the garden of Gethsemane Jesus prayed, "Not my will, but thine be done." How many of us would dare make such a statement? What if God really made a demand upon your life? Could you say, "Thy will be done?" Calvary is only one thing, sacrifice. Giving, giving and giving again. Giving your life, your total life, all of life to the Lord Jesus Christ. I ask you to bow in His eternal presence as I pray.

Almighty God, I pray for those of this audience who are bowing in Thy presence. May they know the joys of salvation through the shed blood of Jesus Christ. May they be willing to surrender all to Thee. In Thy name I pray. Amen.

27 — Harvest Time

Recently David Wilkerson has written a book entitled Jesus Christ–Solid Rock. In this publication he talks about the harvest of the end time, and on today's broadcast of "Christ in the Now" I want to share some of the excerpts from this book. He states, "Jesus Christ is now the only solid ground left in a sinking, dying world. In the Bible, Jesus refers to believers as His 'Bride.' While still on earth He pinpointed a time in history he would return to 'capture' his bride from the earth. That hour has come! Any moment now, night or day, millions will suddenly disappear. It will happen in the twinkling of an eye, in fact, in a split second. Every true Jesus person will vanish from the earth to meet Jesus Christ in the celestial Heavens, leaving a shocked world behind. This is no joke; it is not a fantasy; it is the absolute truth! Jesus Christ is coming soon. He gave certain signs to prove His coming was right at the door! The world has witnessed the fulfillment of these signs. The world is in its midnight hour, and who can honestly deny it? And so a cry is now being made: Behold, Jesus Christ, the bridegroom is coming for His bride! God predicted a Jesus restoration movement just before the end and that spirit outpouring is right now sweeping the earth. It is the last sign, the last call, the last conviction."

Ladies and gentlemen these words from this publication points us very vividly to the truth of the nearness of the coming of Jesus and the gathering of the righteous harvest. James admonishes the Church to "be patient, waiting for the coming of the Lord," just like the farmer waits for his harvest. According to the Scriptures before harvest, there must be an early and a latter rain. Therefore, be patient, be established in your hearts, for the coming of the Lord is near. Finally, to you Christians, who are laboring for the Lord, remember that the Bible states that "He that goeth forth and weepeth, bearing precious seed, shall doubtless come again with rejoicing, bringing his sheaves with him." Yes, I believe it's harvest time and the harvest will be quite sudden. The harvest is absolutely necessary. To the unsaved of this audience, let me ask, "Are you a part of this harvest?" You can be and I ask you to bow in the eternal presence of the Lord as I pray for your salvation.

Almighty God, recognizing it's harvest time, let us be aware as never before of the nearness of the coming of Thy Son. Save those who are bowing in Thy presence right now. In Thy name I pray. Amen.

28 — The Glorious Transformation

This old world of ours has been the stage of many wonderful events. It was a great event when God spoke the world into existence. It was a memorable night when the Heavens suddenly became aglow with the glory of God and the angel choir sang above the green fields of Bethlehem the sweet song that Christ had come into the world. And there have been wonderful events in all succeeding time.

But, in this message I am going to tell you about an event that is yet future. This event is more wonderful than all the events that have taken place before now. This event is the Lord's coming again!

The Apostle Paul graphically relates this event in I Thessalonians 4 when he says, "For the Lord Himself shall descend from Heaven, with a shout, with the blast of the trumpet of God and the dead in Christ shall rise first, then, we which are alive and remain shall be caught up to be with the Lord in the air, and so shall we ever be with the Lord!"

If you are a Christian, this event will mean many wonderful things. First, it will mean that since we are part of the body of Christ, we are heirs of everything that it implies. The body of Christ is the Church and it is bounded on one side by Pentecost and on the other by the Second Coming of Christ. And if you are a child of God you are going to be favored in a way that even Abraham and David and all of the Old Testament saints are not, because you accepted Christ and have been redeemed by the precious blood of Christ. The one who accepts Christ now will be one of the most favored beings in the universe of God.

Secondly, when Christ returns, the Christian is going to get his reward! That is what Paul meant when he said, "Henceforth there is laid up for me a crown of righteousness which the Lord, the righteous judge shall give me at that day; and not to me only but unto all them also that love His appearing." The Scriptures teach that we are going to be like Him and that's part of the reward. "When He shall appear, we shall be like Him for we shall see Him as He is." The changed body will be glorious, but the soul will at last be made perfect and be like the soul of Jesus.

Thirdly, His coming means the reunion of loved ones that have died in the faith! Paul told the Thessalonians to stop worrying over those who died in the faith for "If they are asleep in Jesus, they will be with Him when He comes, for the dead in Christ shall rise first and together we will go and be with the Lord." This also means that some of us may never have to die. For every true child of God who is alive at the coming of Christ will be caught up without dying. The Bible says, "Behold, I shew you a mystery, we shall not all sleep but we shall all be changed. In a moment, in the twinkling of an eye, at the last trump; for the trumpet shall sound and the dead shall be raised incorruptible, and we shall all be changed." This means that this poor, crumbling tabernacle of clay will be changed in the twinkling of an eye into the likeness of Christ's own glorious body.

And lo, suddenly, in the twinkling of an eye, when Jesus comes, the palsy is gone, the disease is swallowed up, the mind is touched with the illuminating finger of God and wrinkles and pains and aches and mental ravings will be gone forever!

In closing, let us note that the Bible says, "Be ye therefore also ready, for in such an hour as ye think not the Son of Man cometh." Think what this will mean to the person who is not a Christian. He is left behind to go through the great tribulation and to suffer the wrath of God. I would like to ask you this morning, "Should His coming take place now, would you go with Him or would you be left behind?" Let us pray.

Almighty God, we enter Thy presence with thanksgiving for this glorious hope of the soon return of Thy son! Yet, we realize there are those listening to this ministry that are nor prepared. I pray that Thy Holy Spirit shall touch their hearts right now. Save and make them ready for Thy coming. I pray in the name of Christ. Amen.

29 — Inevitable Encounters

We live in an hour when people are trying to escape the realities of life, retreating into an imaginary world. Instead of facing the realities of life, they are trying to hide in an illusive, imaginary world. But man sooner or later must face up to the realities of God, sin and the judgement. The Bible says, "How shall we escape if we neglect so great a salvation." One may drown his troubles in alcohol, another may drift off into some dream world, while some even commit suicide.

All of these are the tricks of the devil because one of his great designs and plans is that you get a measure of temporary satisfaction out of what you are doing. The Bible speaks of people who, "became vain in their imaginations and their foolish heart was darkened." Satan is described as an "angel of light" and he does a good job of selling the unreal.

He succeeded in getting Samson to trade his real power and strength for the imagination of passion and desire. The prodigal son imagined that the pleasures of the far off country were greater than the joys of his home. After wasting his substance in riotous living, he returned to his father in repentance and tears and begged to be a hired servant in his father's house.

My friend, it is time to face the realities of life, the inevitable things, things that are going to come our way. I know that it is hard to do, but before I finish this message I want to show you how it is possible.

There are three indisputable facts you must face. The first one is the fact that YOU MUST DIE! Death is the sentence hanging over every one of us for the Bible says, "It is appointed unto men once to die." Everyone listening to me today has an appointment with death. No one knows the exact moment they are going to cross the precipice into eternity. The Bible says, "What is your life? It is even a vapour that appeareth for a little while and then vanished away."

We have no promise of tomorrow. When the summons comes, no one has the power to stay. The answer as to how you are going to die is up to you. It's a terrifying moment to look back and know with sobering conviction that you've missed it, that your life has been all wrong, and that you have completely missed the mark and that you have no plea to make as you face judgement.

Death is an honest moment; it cannot be bribed. It's verdict is final; there can be no appeal. You have finished your test and handed in your paper. There is nothing you can erase and the wrong answer you have given must stand for eternity.

My friends, it's a bad thing for a sinner to die. And then after death you must face this second fact that you MUST MEET GOD. The Bible says, "...everyone of us shall give account of himself to God...none of us liveth to himself, and no man dieth to himself." At the end of the road you will find God waiting for you because death does not end it all. The Bible says, "After death the judgement." The Bible says, "Prepare to meet Thy God." The Lord has decreed that every man shall give account of himself to God. This decree is certain. All men must face God in judgement.

The third fact you cannot get around is that YOU ARE GOING TO SPEND ETERNITY SOMEWHERE. The immortal question rings out, "If a man die shall he live again." The answer is yes, because there is an eternity to face and even though you would destroy your body, the soul will live throughout eternity. The question that comes into focus relative to eternity is, "where are you going to spend it?" The Bible tells us there are only two places, Heaven or hell. If you want to go to Heaven, you can because the decision is yours. You have Heaven to gain by accepting Jesus Christ as your Savior.

30 — Good News from a Graveyard

In the gospel according to John 11:22, we read a statement made by Martha, the sister of Lazarus. Even though Lazarus had been dead four days, Martha said to Jesus, "But I know that even now, whatsoever thou wilt ask of God, God will give it thee." Her statement in this fatal and final moment showed her faith to be strong and alive. She possessed a living faith that sustained her in this impossible situation. No one could have been more heart broken than Martha. No one's clouds could have been darker, no one's future more lonely, no one's memories more painful, and no one's petition more hopeless from a human point of view. Yet, standing there in conversation with Jesus, amid multitudes of reasons to despair, she expresses faith in Christ and His power to bring anything to pass.

The reason Martha could make a statement of faith like this was because she had a personal relationship with Christ. And the fact that she knew Christ and His power to bring to pass caused hope to spring up with expectancy unexplainable. She knew Him to be the God of creation, the God who spoke into existence all the elements contained in the stone before the tomb and who could remove that stone and bring her brother forth. She knew Him to be the God of the living and the God of the dead, the God of the man of riches or of rags, the God of kings and of the subjects, of the free man and of the prisoner, and the God of the sick and the well. Knowing this, she expected an uneventful visit from Him who had said, "I am the resurrection and the life."

Because of this faith they made the journey again to the tomb of their brother. This time they went with high hopes instead of deep despair and when they returned they brought with them the result of their living faith, a dead brother living again. To be acquainted with Jesus as Martha was is to believe Him to be all sufficient. He is not limited in His power to any particular field but He is able to take care of any need. God specializes in things thought to be impossible.

Ladies and gentlemen, it is never too late to take up a fight in faith against your problems. If Jesus can reach beyond the curtain of death and bring back a dead man and restore him to life and health, there most assuredly is hope for you who are hearing me at this hour. You are not beyond God's reach if you will gather your scattered faith and put it to work against your trouble. One of the greatest joys of being a minister is the privilege of telling helpless and hopeless people that there remains a provision for their lives. Some people get the idea that they have gone too far in their evil practices and that God will not help them. But let me assure you, that God can bring order out of chaos, and that "He came to seek and to save that which was lost." I have no way of knowing what your particular problems and perplexities are. But let me give you renewed hope and courage. Your situation is not hopeless, your problem is not difficult, and you are not beyond God's reach in this hour. Let us say with Martha, "...I know, that even now whatsoever thou wilt ask of God, God will give it thee."

Let us pray. Almighty God, we bow in Thy eternal presence, knowing the all sufficiency of Thy power. I pray for everyone listening to this broadcast right now. Meet their need, whatever it may be, and touch their lives by Thy great power. In Thy name I pray. Amen.

31 — You Can't Always Go with the Tide

In the latter part of the 19th century, England still had a law prohibiting a motor vehicle from exceeding four miles per hour. If a vehicle traveled at this tremendous speed, the law required that a man precede it with a red flag to notify the public of the dangerous invention coming down the road. Today we have means of transportation that travel at more than a hundred times that rate. The crowd was wrong in its evaluation of the motor vehicle and its future role in the nations of the world. And the crowd has been wrong many times since.

The crowd was wrong when they called Westinghouse a fool for daring to think he could stop a railroad train with wind. But today, the Westinghouse Air Brake is used around the world. McCormick was laughed at by the crowd when he invented the first reaper. People derided it as a cross between a chariot, a wheelbarrow, and a flying machine. But the crowd was wrong. F.W. Woolworth was told he had no business ability. His superiors gave him a caretaker's job. But they were wrong. Woolworth's stores are found throughout the world. The mistaken crowd laughed at Goodyear during the 11 years he worked on vulcanizing rubber. But the crowd was mistaken. Vulcanizing has become part of the tire business.

The crowd has often been wrong and in many instances it is wrong today. Especially is the worldly crowd wrong in its attitude towards Christ and the things of God. The Bible says, "Broad is the way that leadeth to destruction and many there be which go in thereat." Are you part of the crowd that is saying, 'Away with Christ?'

Today, though you are wrong about a thousand other things, do not be wrong about spiritual matters. The Bible says, "Enter ye in at the strait gate which leadeth unto life." There is no one better than Christ to follow and believe in. There is no better message in the world than John 3:16 which says, "For God so loved the world, that he gave his only begotten Son, that whosoever believeth in him should not perish, but have everlasting life." There is no more comforting statement than Isaiah 53 which says, "All we like sheep have gone astray; we have turned every one to his own way; but the Lord hath laid on him the iniquity of us all."

You may have to stem the tide of public opinion to follow the Lord. You may have to stand alone. But even if the crowd refuses this invitation for your soul's sake and for the sake of your eternal destination, I ask you to accept and believe it. The Bible says, "Come now, let us reason together, saith the Lord; though your sins be as scarlet, they shall be as white as snow; though they be red like crimson, they shall be as wool."

Today, as we pray, I ask you to bow in the eternal presence of Christ, and commit your life to Him. Let us pray.

Almighty God, giver and sustainer of life, I come to You on behalf of those who are bowing in Thy presence. Come into their hearts; cleanse them from sin, and give them power to stand firmly for their faith in Christ. In Thy name I pray. Amen.

32 — Superman or Super God?

The theme of the Bible is "Jesus." In the Old Testament He is spoken of as one who is coming. As we read the gospels of Matthew, Mark, Luke and John, we have the record of Christ having already come. Then, we turn to the Acts and the Epistles and take note of the fact that He has ascended back to Heaven, but the promise is left that He is coming again.

The greatest name in the world is Jesus. He came to bring life more abundantly. He came to deliver people from their fears and mental illnesses of this life. He came to bring health to both soul and body. And when you hear the story of Jesus, you've heard the greatest story ever uttered from the lips of man.

Jesus of Nazareth came to this earth at the lowest tide in the history of man. He came in the fading, flickering light of the old Law of Moses. He stepped into a river of water, was baptized by man, then He climbed the banks of that river and started towards the human race as fast as He could. His steps led to Galilee and within a matter of days He had released energy, ideals and power into human society that are still as fresh and current as the day He first uttered them. Within a matter of weeks Jesus had crashed the headlines of the world. Within a matter of months, the human race was dizzy with the momentum and excitement of this man as he captured the imagination of all mankind.

As Christ walked the rocky shores of Galilee He turned them into the main streets of the world. The multitude thronged Him on every side to see the miracles that He did. They came to see Him who was perfect in strength for Christ never knew sickness and disease never marred His flesh. His body was so strong that thousands could touch Him and healing flowed out of Him and made them whole. In His mind, Christ had perfect intelligence and wisdom. He knew and understood all things as He discerned the hearts of men. This perfect wisdom and knowledge radiated itself everywhere and even when His enemies tried to trap Him in His words they were unsuccessful. The Spirit of Jesus Christ was perfect love because He did nothing but that which would save people or heal their broken, maimed, sick bodies and their troubled minds. He came to fill men with goodness and to make them the kind of people they ought to be.

He was too wise to do wrong and too good to make a mistake. When Christ spoke it was as one with authority and commandment. His voice thrilled little children, comforted and strengthened the old. He spoke two words to Matthew, a tax collector and he left all and followed Jesus. He stood on ship and said, "Peace be still," and the winds and waves obeyed His command. Then, as He touched the people it was with perfect power. He touched blind eyes and they were opened. He touched the tongues of the dumb and they talked. He touched the ears that had never heard and they were able to hear. He touched paralytics and they leaped and walked. He even touched a dead child and it was raised back to life.

These are but a few of the great things that Jesus did while here on earth. Yet, the Bible says in Hebrews 13:8, "Jesus Christ is the same yesterday, today and forever." His power is real today and He can still touch your life. This very moment by exercising faith in the Son of God, His divine power can be manifested in your life. For Jesus says, "Come unto me all ye that labour and are heavy laden, and I will give you rest." Again He said, "Him that cometh to me, I will in no wise cast out."

Ladies and gentlemen, if right now you will bow in the presence of the eternal Christ He can make you whole. He can mend that broken heart. He can restore health to your life and He can lift you from the valley of despair and despondency and you can begin life anew.

Let us pray. Almighty God, we bow in the presence of Thy Son, Jesus Christ, with a sincere desire to feel the touch of His wonderful power. We pray that right now His holy presence shall fill the heart of every one listening to this radio ministry. Heal the sick, save the lost, deliver the ones who are bound by fear and illusions. We pray in Thy name. Amen.

33 — Gimme' That Old Time Religion!

It was divine inspiration alone that caused the Old Testament Prophet Daniel to predict that in the last days, "knowledge shall be increased." Someone has said that "If Adam had lived until the day I was born, and if he had died on the day of my birth, then I would still have seen more change and more technical advance in my lifetime than Adam would have seen in nearly six millenniums."

In just a few years we have gone from kerosene lamps to the laser beam, from the pony express to instant worldwide television. We live in a day when transplanting vital organs from one body to another is common. Things that we call ordinary "necessities of life" are things that kings never dreamed of a few years ago. We are always thankful for any extra luxury that we can have, and none of us care to go back to those days that are so pleasant to talk about. We even do all that we can to see to it that our children do not have to know the hardships we knew. But I'm wondering if our world hasn't allowed the "cares of this life" to rob us of that one old fashioned blessing we need and that is a religious experience that touches and changes the heart and life.

Men are getting so intelligent that they think they don't need God anymore. They tell us that He is dead, that old time religion was all right for a primitive people who didn't know any better, but in our enlightened age we have grown beyond the need for emotionalism in religion.

Recently, Pat Boone was asked on the Merv Griffin TV Show, the reason for the tremendous religious change that has been brought about in his life. Pat Boone said, "I learned the difference between religion and relationship."

Ladies and gentlemen, I believe that when an individual comes into a vital relationship with Jesus Christ there will be a tremendous change in their life. I feel that we need more preaching of the gospel that produces something you can feel. We need more "godly sorrow that worketh repentance." Tears of conviction flowing down the face of sinners would be a blessing to any church. I do not feel we have to go back to the days of tallow candles to have heart felt religion. God and His Bible have not changed. The Apostle Paul prayed for the church in Corinth that they would not be soon removed from the simplicity that there is in Christ Jesus. That same Apostle said, "If I have all knowledge...and have not love; it profiteth me nothing."

We should never let our heads get ahead of our hearts in that which pertains to a relationship with Christ. We need the love and the old time religion that "passeth understanding." In times like these you need a Savior. One you can put your faith and trust in. One who can still the storms and tempests of your life. And that Savior is Jesus Christ who can completely transform and change your life. I ask you to bow in His eternal presence right now, open your heart to Him and let Him come in.

Let us pray. Almighty God, giver of Thy Son, Jesus Christ, we bow in Thy presence with grateful hearts. We know that Thy presence in our lives can change and transform. Make us to know afresh and anew the wonderful salvation you can bring into a life. In Thy name I pray. Amen.

34 — I Shall Return

In the dark days of 1942, as the enemy forces tightened their grip on the Philippine Islands, General Douglas MacArthur had to withdraw; but, before he departed he gave his Filipino friends a promise. He said, "I shall return." And history records that he kept his word. He directed the victorious sweep of the American forces as they fought back across the Pacific and then he appeared in person.

It was a dramatic moment when the general dressed in his familiar field uniform, waded ashore at Manila and announced, "I have returned." One of the most precious statements in the entire Bible is the promise Christ made to his Disciples: "I will come again." We are still waiting for His return, but the "signs of the times" lead us to believe His Second Coming will be very soon.

When Jesus was ascending back to Heaven, the apostles watched Him go up and as He disappeared from their sight they heard the angels say: "Ye men of Galilee, why stand ye gazing up into Heaven? This same Jesus, which is taken up from you into Heaven, shall so come in like manner as ye have seen Him go into Heaven." (Acts 1:11) This reminded the apostles of His promise to "come again" and assured them that He would return in a cloud just as He had ascended in a cloud and that He would come back in a bodily form.

As we read the New Testament we note that it is full of references to the Second Coming of Christ. It teaches that first He will come secretly and take away all the born again Christians who are ready to go into Heaven with Him and that soon afterward He will make a great public appearance when "every eye shall see Him."

The pattern of His Second Coming is given very clearly in I Thessalonians 4:16–17, "For the Lord himself shall descend from Heaven with a shout, with the voice of the archangel, and with the trump of God: and the dead in Christ shall rise first: Then we which are alive and remain shall be caught up together with them in the clouds, to meet the Lord in the air: and so shall we ever be with the Lord."

The coming of Christ will produce a twofold effect. It will cause great joy among the righteous, who suddenly will leave all the troubles of this life behind them. Sorrow, pain, disfigurement, and death shall be known to them no more. But, on the other hand, it will mean terror for all that do not love the Lord. The Bible teaches that Christ is going to make war against His enemies and become ruler over all the world. According to the Scriptures this event could take place at any time. Jesus said, "Be ye therefore ready also; for the Son of Man cometh at an hour when ye think not."

There will be no advance warning to give anyone time to get ready. Those who are wise will get ready now by turning away from all sin in heartfelt repentance and by trusting in Christ as their personal Savior. All mankind is divided into two classes: those who are ready and those who are not. Those who have asked God for a clean heart and a new life will arise to meet the Lord when He comes. Those who have refused to be saved will be left behind to suffer with the ungodly.

Ladies and gentlemen, which class are you in today? I beg of you, right now, to turn to God with all of your heart and let Christ come in.

Let us pray. Almighty God, giver and sustainer of life, I pray for the unsaved of this audience who are not ready for the coming of Thy Son, Jesus Christ. Help them to know the hour is very near at hand and that they must prepare for this great event. I pray for those who are bowing in Thy presence. Come into their hearts and make them thine. In Thy name I pray. Amen.

35 — Thanksgiving is Good, Thanks-living Better!

America has a holiday that is not celebrated in every part of the world and this week we celebrate that day. Thanksgiving Day is a day set apart to give thanks to God for His many blessings bestowed upon our lives. The Bible admonishes us to be thankful for it states: "...with Thanksgiving, let your request be made known to God." The Scriptures enjoin us to come before the Lord with thanksgiving. In this message today I want to share with you several things that thanksgiving means to me.

First, Thanksgiving means thoughtfulness. The words "think" and "thank" come from the same Anglo-Saxon word which lets us know that we are not thankful until we are thoughtful. If you are really thankful, you should begin to count your blessings and express such to the great God of this universe for the Bible says, "every good and every perfect gift comes from above."

The second thing Thanksgiving means to me is appreciation. I believe we would be more thankful if we were less fault finding. Instead of thinking negatively at this season of the year, let us think of the good things of life and be appreciative of what we have instead of complaining about what we don't have.

Thirdly, Thanksgiving means Thanks-saying. A well known commercial says, "Say it with flowers." But, it is also well to express our thanks with words. The Bible says, "Out of the abundance of the heart the mouth speaketh." During this Thanksgiving week, I suggest that each one listening to this message call or better yet go and see someone who has been a blessing or inspiration to you and say to them, "I appreciate you. You are a blessing to me." But most of all, let us tell God how much we love and appreciate him.

Fourth, I believe Thanksgiving means Thanks-doing. Someone has said, "Words are proper, but deeds are better." The Bible says, "And whatsoever ye do in word or deed, do all in the name of the Lord Jesus, giving thanks to God and the Father by Him." Psalms 50:14 admonishes: "Offer unto God thanksgiving: and pay thy vows unto the most High." If we are really thankful, we are going to do something about it. If we are thankful for health then we are going to expend our energies in the work of the Lord. If we are thankful that we live in America we are going to attend God's House and thank Him for this privilege. If we are truly thankful for the financial blessings of this life, then, we are going to share so that others can be blessed as we have been.

Yes, Thanksgiving means Thanks-doing. Thanksgiving is a privilege as well as a duty and as such should be spontaneous, perennial and enthusiastic. Thanks from the heart should be expressed definitely, unceasingly.

The story is told of a man by the name of Henry Dorsey Gough who was a wealthy Maryland planter of the days of slavery who experienced an incident in his life that made him more thankful. While riding one day to one of his plantations, he heard the voice of prayer and praise in a cabin. As he listened he discovered that a slave from another estate was leading the devotions of his own slaves and offering fervent thanksgiving for all the blessings of their depressed lot. His heart was touched with emotion, and he exclaimed: "O Lord! I have many thousands, and yet, ungrateful wretch that I am. I never thank Thee, as this poor slave does. He has scarcely clothes to put on, or food to satisfy his hunger. I have plenty, shame on me, Lord, for being unthankful."

If we begin to count our many blessings of the present and meditate upon the glory of God, if we endeavor to forget the unpleasant things and consider the great fact of redemption through Christ, our hearts will be filled with thanksgiving unto our "Bountiful God."

Let us pray. Almighty God, giver and sustainer of life, we lift our hearts to Thee in praise and gratitude for Thy many blessings. Forgive our selfishness and show Thy way of love and blessing. In Thy name I pray. Amen.

36 Part 1 — The Holy City

Jerusalem is the most religious centered city on the face of the earth. When we consider that three of the great world religions were born there, we come to understand why it is unprecedented in religious fervor and religious violence. The very name Jerusalem seems a mockery. It bears the name of peace and yet more blood has been shed per square foot in the environs of Jerusalem than in any other city in history. Men and devils have been determined to destroy its name from the face of the earth and yet it stands at this moment as almost the Mistress of peace on earth. One wrong step in Jerusalem today and a World War III holocaust would break upon the nations of the world. Not only are there vigorous religions making demands upon this Holy City, but the greatest military giants of world history are watching over her like a witch watching a boiling pot.

While all world empires of history have sought to determine the destiny of Jerusalem, modern nations such as the United States and Soviet Russia feel a destiny in their decisions regarding Jerusalem. What the world must know is that God has predetermined not only the destiny of Jerusalem but the events leading to its destiny. In this message I want to briefly list eight prophetic events yet to come to the city of Jerusalem, four today and four next Sunday.

First, Jerusalem Will Be Besieged By World Armies

In Zechariah 12:3 God says the armies will be gathered against Jerusalem. Also, Chapter 14:2 states, "For I will gather all nations against Jerusalem to battle." Prophecy being true, the war over Jerusalem is not over. The bloodshed in Jerusalem is not finished. We must always remember that the devil hates Jerusalem because it is where the Savior of the world died. It was where God made His great promises to Abraham and it was there the Church was born.

Secondly, Jerusalem Will Be A Global Burden

God says in Zechariah 12:2. "I will make Jerusalem a cup of trembling unto all the people round about, when they shall be in the siege both against Judah and against Jerusalem." Before the United Nations and every other political body on earth Jerusalem is now a cup of trembling. It holds the key to peace or war. Zechariah 12:3 states, "And in that day will I make Jerusalem a burdensome stone for all people: all that burden themselves with it shall be cut in pieces, though all the people of the earth be gathered against it." The prophet saw the titanic end time struggle preceding the Second Coming of the Lord Jesus Christ when all nations will be gathered against Jerusalem. God has said that the city is a burdensome stone. This means it is so heavy that people cannot carry the problems of Jerusalem. And God predicts He will cut in pieces those who gather against it.

Thirdly, The Prince Of Peace, Jesus Christ, Will Personally Intervene In Jerusalem

Zechariah 14:3-4 states, "Then shall the Lord go forth, and fight against those nations, as when he fought in the day of battle. And his feet shall stand in that day upon the Mount of Olives, which is before Jerusalem on the east, and the Mount of Olives shall cleave in the midst thereof toward the east and toward the west, and there shall be a very great valley; and half of the mountain shall remove toward the north, and half of it toward the south." In the wars of recent years it has been an overwhelming fact that though Israel had amazing odds against her small fighting forces it was miraculous how she won her battle. In the Bible, many times God fought for the people of Israel in the field of battle to preserve them. And God has promised that at Jerusalem He would do this again.

Fourth, The Messiah Will Be Revealed To Israel At Jerusalem

Zechariah 12:10 states: "I will pour upon the house of David, and upon the inhabitants of Jerusalem, the spirit of grace and of supplications: and they shall look upon me whom they have pierced, and they shall mourn for him, as one mourneth for his only son, and shall be in bitterness for him, as one that is in bitterness for his firstborn." In the rest of this chapter God explains how the people of Jerusalem and Israel shall mourn when they come to know that Jesus Christ is truly the Messiah. As prophesied here, when they look upon Him whom they have "pierced," what an amazing fact will be theirs when they actually see the nail pierced hands and He says, "I received these from your forefathers." At that time there will be mourning in Jerusalem such as the nation has never known before. Their mourning will make up for 2,000 years of waywardness against God. It will be the greatest mourning in history when an entire nation mourns because of the sins of its forefathers and seeks peace with the Messiah and seeks reclamation from God.

Ladies and gentlemen, God is working on a timetable. If you want to know how up-to-date the Bible is, read the prophecies concerning Israel and Jerusalem, and see how they correlate with your newspaper. If you are not prepared for the Second Coming of Christ, now is the time to prepare. His coming is very near at hand, even at the door and the time to get ready is now.

Let us pray. Almighty God, giver and sustainer of life, I pray for those who are bowing in Thy presence. Come into their hearts, cleanse them from sin and make them whole by Thy great and wonderful power. Make them ready for Thy coming. In Thy name I pray. Amen.

36 Part 2 — The New Jerusalem

Last Sunday on the "Christ in the Now" broadcast I presented the first of a two part message entitled "Eight Prophetic Events facing Jerusalem." In that message I listed four of them. They are:

1. Jerusalem will be besieged by world armies as noted in Zechariah 12 and 14.
2. Jerusalem will be a global burden as stated in Zachariah 12:2.
3. Zechariah 14:3-4 states that the Prince of Peace, Jesus Christ, will personally intervene in Jerusalem.
4. The Messiah will be revealed to Israel at Jerusalem as prophesied in Zechariah 12:10.

Today, I list four other prophecies concerning Jerusalem.

Fifth, Israel Will Sorrow Because Of the Crucifixion of Christ

We have record of this in Zechariah 12:11-12 and Zechariah 13:6-7. It states: "And one shall say unto him, 'What are these wounds in thine hands?' Then he shall answer, 'Those with which I was wounded in the house of my friends.'" When this astounding revelation comes to Israel, they will have great sorrow because of the crucifixion of Christ. There will be national mourning.

The Sixth Prophecy Concerning Israel Has To Do With The Fountain Of Cleansing And Healing Being Opened In Jerusalem

Zechariah 13:1 says, "In that day there shall be a fountain opened to the house of David and to the inhabitants of Jerusalem for sin and for uncleanness." Verse 2 says, "And it shall come to pass in that day, saith the Lord of hosts, that I will cut off the name of the idols out of the land, and they shall no more be remembered: and also I will cause the prophets and the unclean spirit to pass out of the land." All cultic followings shall disappear from that land. The various cults scattered throughout the land shall be taken out. And God says they shall not only be taken out but they shall be remembered no more. God has proclaimed that a clean spirit will pass throughout the land.

The Seventh Prophecy Concerning Jerusalem Has To Do With The Fact That Christ Shall Return To Jerusalem.

Zechariah 14:4 says, "And his feet shall stand in that day upon the Mount of Olives, which is before Jerusalem on the east." Christ's return shall bring a new day into all the earth for the Scriptures declare, "And it shall be in that day, that living waters shall go out from Jerusalem." Jerusalem shall then be the center of world worship. Zechariah 14:16 says, "And it shall come to pass, that every one that is left of all the nations which came against Jerusalem shall even go up from year to year to worship the King, the Lord of hosts, and to keep the Feast of Tabernacles." At that time Jerusalem will be a universal religious center where Christ Himself shall reign.

The Eighth And Last Prophecy Of This Message Is That The Millenial Kingdom Will Be At Jerusalem.

Zechariah 14:9 says, "And the Lord shall be king over all the earth: in that day shall there be one Lord, and his name one." Then in verse 11 we note: "And men shall dwell in it, and there shall be no more utter destruction; but Jerusalem shall be safely inhabited." The Scriptures declare that God shall bring great wealth to Jerusalem. "And Judah also shall fight at Jerusalem: and the wealth of all the heathen round about shall be gathered together, gold and silver, and apparel, in great abundance." For one thousand years Jesus Christ shall reign from Jerusalem.

Ladies and gentlemen, God has a timetable. It has been posted for centuries. He has a time and a place to deal with Jerusalem. Are you ready for His coming? If not, bow in His presence as we pray.

Almighty God, I bow in Thy presence, offering prayer for these of this radio audience who have heard this message concerning the prophetic events which are to take place concerning Jerusalem and yet, are not ready for Thy coming. Save them now, let them experience the joys of salvation. In Thy name I pray. Amen.

37 — Born Once, Die Twice; Born Twice, Die Once!

In John 3 we have the record of the conversation of Jesus and Nicodemus concerning the New Birth. Jesus said, "Except a man be born again, he cannot see the kingdom of God." He further stated, "The wind bloweth where it listeth and so is everyone that is born of the Spirit." This literally means that while we cannot tell whence the wind comes or where it goes, we can hear and feel it and see its effects. Let us examine some of these effects of the Divine Wind on human life and consider some of the meanings of the New Birth.

FIRST, the New Birth removes all guilt of sin from the mind and heart, resulting in a clear conscience. The Bible says, "How much more shall the blood of Christ...purge your conscience from dead works to serve the living God." The accumulated load of repeated transgressions in the life of the sinner creates an ever growing pyramid of guilt that becomes almost unbearable. When the penalty for his sin was pronounced upon Cain, he cried with despair, "My punishment is greater than I can bear." David also voiced the distress of the sinner when he cried, "For mine iniquities are gone over mine head: as a heavy burden they are too heavy for me." But in the New Birth all this is changed. Only the twice-born can understand the accuracy and the reality of the old hymn, "At the Cross, at the Cross, where I first saw the light, and the burden of my heart rolled away." Because this is exactly what happens, the burden of sin is lifted, the heavy heart is made light, and the conscience is made crystal clear.

SECOND, the New Birth makes possible a clean life. If the New Birth makes possible a clean life, and if the New Birth meant only the pardoning of past transgressions, it would fail to meet human need, for the sinful nature with all its evil desires and actions would still be intact. But thanks be to God, the forgiveness of the past is only part of the salvation that Christ offers. He breaks the power of canceled sin, and sets the prisoners free. The heart is changed, the desires are purged, and the inward thought pattern is broken and recast in conformity with God's will, thus making possible a clean life through Christ.

THIRD, the New Birth also purges the record of sin from God's Word. The fact that a record of individual sins is kept by God is clearly shown in Revelation 20:12 which says, "And I saw the dead, small and great, stand before God: and the books were opened...and the dead were judged out of those things which were found written in the books, according to their works." But how marvelous is the grace that God extends to purge the guilty record for all that accept Jesus Christ as their Savior. God has said, "I have blotted out as a thick cloud thy transgressions and their sins and iniquities will I remember no more." This divine "blotting out" and "forgetting" of sin is most assuredly one of the glorious fruits and benefits of the New Birth. Today, Jesus Christ can transform your life by His mighty power. The New Birth can become a reality in your life. You can know the joys of sins forgiven and the peace of God that "passeth understanding" can flood and thrill your heart and life. I ask you to bow in the eternal presence of the Christ of Calvary and let Him come into your heart.

Let us pray. Almighty God, giver and sustainer of life, I bow in Thy presence with thanksgiving because you have made possible the wonderful New Birth through Thy Son, Jesus Christ. I pray that each one who has heard this message today, that is not born again, may know the wonderful saving grace of God in their lives. In Thy name, I pray. Amen.

38 — Promises, Promises, Promises!

On today's "Christ in The Now" broadcast I would like to speak to you of "The Magnitude of God's Promises." As we look into the Scriptures we note that the promises of God are of such magnitude that their fulfillment oft times span generations and even centuries. The Bible states in the Old Testament, "the vision is yet for an appointed time...though it tarry, wait for it, because it will surely come." Again we read the admonition, "Cast not away your confidence, that after ye have done the will of God, ye might receive the promise."

The Scriptures pictures the greatness of God in Ephesians 3:20 when it states: "Unto Him that is able to do exceeding abundantly above all that we ask or think." I would like to look at some of the promises of God and their fulfillment so that our confidence can be inspired that we could appropriate the right promises to our lives.

First, let us look at God's promises to Abraham. God promised him all the land from the Euphrates to the Nile. He promised that his seed would be as the stars of Heaven and he was also promised a city whose builder and maker is God. These promises Abraham did not live to see fulfilled but he embraced them. And even today the consummation of some of them is still unfolding.

Then we note that God through the prophet Joel promised to some day pour out His Spirit upon all flesh. That promise began to be fulfilled at Pentecost and we are enjoying a portion of the promise today as we see the mighty outpouring of God's spirit. The promise of God, through his servant Haggai, to disturb the universe found partial fulfillment in Christ's first advent. At His birth there was the brilliant star, the angelic choir, and Heaven's consternation that the jewel of that expanse was departing. Then, at His death, there was the rending of the earth, the blackened sun, supernatural darkness, ten thousand angels held on a leash, and heartbroken God. Even Haggai's promise is yet to have its final chapter when Christ comes again.

With these promises of God in mind, let me note with you three promises that you can appropriate to your life today. First, if you are in need of salvation the Lord has promised to save all that come to Him. The Scriptures declare that "He will in no wise refuse those to come to him for salvation." In fact, the Bible states, "Whosoever shall call upon the name of the Lord shall be saved." Second, there is the promise of God for healing. The Bible states: "I am the Lord Thy God that healeth thee" and again the Scripture promises that "these signs shall follow them that believe...they shall lay hands on the sick and they shall recover."

Thirdly, God has promised abundant life. Jesus said in John 10:10, "The thief (that is, the devil) cometh to steal, to kill, and to destroy. But I am come that you might have abundant life."

Again the promise is made in the Scriptures, "Beloved, I wish above all things that thou mayest prosper and be in health, even as thy soul prospereth."

This is available to you in the now. Ladies and gentlemen, let me admonish you to appropriate the promises of God to your life. There is a promise for every need and if you will by faith cling to what God has promised in His Word you can know the wonderful fulfillment of God's Word in your life.

Let us pray. Almighty God, I enter Thy presence on the promise that Jesus made when he was on earth. He said: "Whatsoever thou asketh the Father in my name shall be done." We ask that these promises be fulfilled in the lives of those who are bowing in Thy presence. Save the unsaved, heal the sick, and give abundant life to those who ask. In Thy name I pray. Amen.

39 — God in a Baby

No one can possibly know the depths of the mysteries that surround the adorable person of our Lord Jesus. He stands alone as the eternal, supreme and everlasting God. In my message I want to contemplate the mystery of our God. The Father of Eternity became a child of time. The infinite one became an infant. He, who lived in Heaven without a mother, lived on earth without a Father. He, whom the Heaven of Heavens could not contain, took up residence in the bosom of His virgin mother. The Eternal Spirit took on a body of human flesh. The One who holds the oceans in His hands pled for a drop of water as He hung on the Cross. He, who sustains and upholds all, fell under the mysterious load in Gethsemane. He, whom ten thousands times ten thousands of angels would worship and serve, begged for just one hour of watchful fellowship from his sleeping disciples. The Creator of all plant life grew the tree upon which He died.

As we look at Bethlehem we see the only comprehensible view of God ever given. We see God in a manger, God on Mary's breast. We see the Eternal and Immortal One as He enters the world He created through the gateway of the virgin's womb. He was God manifest in the flesh.

At Bethlehem God became what He was not before and yet He did not cease being what He always was. This dual life is constantly in view. He is both the offerer and the offering, the altar and the sacrifice upon the altar. He is both the Judge and the condemned One. He levies the penalty and then pays it. He demands blood for man's sin and then gives His own for man's redemption. He is just and the justifier of all that believe.

God had manifested Himself in the Creation of Heaven and earth, on Mount Sinai, and in the Tabernacle. His wonders had been seen, His voice heard, His form traced, but He remained invisible, untouchable and unapproachable.

Yet He came into the world and was manifest in the flesh. God walked and talked with men. He healed and loved, blessed and saved, bore our sins in His own body and died for these sins. By the power of the Spirit He emerged from the prison of Joseph's tomb to announce, "Behold, I am alive forevermore."

This is the God He became. He became what I was in sin that I might be like Him in His total righteousness. He came to where I was that I might be where He is. He took upon Himself human form that His divine likeness might be mine forever. He became a curse that I might be justified.

Yes, He was God in the likeness of sinful flesh, bearing my sin in his own body on the tree, and yet He is without sin.

I know this is a mystery. It is awesome, sublime, overwhelming and incomprehensible. Yet, He would not be God if He were not more than we can think Him to be. He is enough for us that the angel could say, "Thou shalt call His name, Immanuel, which means 'God with us.'"

As we face the New Year this is our strength, our hope, and our song–God with us. We close out the dying year and embrace the unseen challenges of the New Year with the solemn, yet glorious assurance that He is our Immanuel, God with us. If you do not have this God in your heart, let Him come in. He said: "Behold, I stand at the door and knock: If any man hear my voice, and open the door, I will come in to him."

Let us pray. Almighty God, we bow in the presence of the eternal and holy God thanking Thee for the provision of Salvation. I pray for those who bow in Thy presence right now. Save them by Thy power. I pray in Thy name. Amen.

40 — The Unavoidable Appointment

Death is a mighty monarch that reigns in the world. Seated upon the pale horse, he has crossed the annals of time and invaded every home, palace, and hut alike. He has no respect for riches, poverty, position or reputation. He has every man on the list as a prospect. Death has dug a trench around the world and filled it with men of every size and color. Death is the skeleton in every man's closet of hope, and the nightmare of every dream. His music is the sobbing of the broken hearted and his fountains are the tears of orphans and widows. His reign is supreme and only two men in all the history of the world have evaded him. Every minute that goes by marks the death of ninety people and five thousand every hour pass out of this life.

The Bible says that Death came by one man's offence. God created man perfect and according to His own image and likeness, and put him over everything in the Garden of Eden. In this Garden everything was perfect and beautiful. There were no falling leaves, no dying grass or fading flowers. Death was not seen in any form or fashion because death was not God's desire for any of His creation. He desired for His creation the continuance of everything pleasant and blissful.

Death is another fact of life that we don't understand but to which we have to submit. Many have foolishly said they would not accept salvation because they couldn't understand it. I am sure we understand as much about salvation as we do about death; yet death is inevitable and this makes salvation essential.

We must make peace with God and leave the things we don't understand in His merciful hands. You can stand and ask questions until you have run out of time and still not get the answer. There is a mystery that lingers over the grave that none can explain. Though death's work is performed in our presence every day and its dominion extends throughout all the world, it's like a cloud hanging low. Yet none on earth have the power to command it to be expelled.

There is a natural desire to escape death even though it takes us into the very presence of God in a split second. Even Jesus said: "Father, if it be possible let this cup pass from me." Every conscious man shudders at the thought, the soulless beast shrinks back and the unconscious member of the vegetable kingdom would resist that which would wither its bloom and destroy its beauty.

None enjoys a feeling of helplessness and all men are rendered so in the presence of death. Kings lay their crowns at their feet, the politician gives up his position, the banker turns over his money, the socialite releases to another her standing in the circle. The judge turns in his gavel and the general his uniform. The poor man leaves his debts and a broken family.

This will be a terrible experience for the backslider. The clearer the view a man has of Christ the greater the anguish when he is forever separated from Him He once had life in his grasp. Turning loose to take what briefly seemed more appealing will cause eternal remorse. The backslider who willfully returned to sin will hate himself throughout eternity finding no escape from a christless doom. The sinner who has never known God will likewise fill a hopeless place in eternity as death takes from him any possible chance of repentance.

But to the Christian hope remains at death. It is not the end of everything but the beginning of a life in glory. Reason says man should live again. Science says man may live again. Philosophy says man wants to live again. Love says I must live again. But Jesus said, "I shall live again." The Christian lays down his cross to receive a crown. He gets a trumpet for his tribulation. He has no problem but eternal peace, no sickness but perfect health. Instead of weakness he receives power and glory.

The song writer has penned the words: "This robe of flesh I'll drop and rise to seize the everlasting prize and shout while passing through the air, farewell, farewell, sweet hour of prayer."

Ladies and Gentlemen, when death grips your life, can you have a peace in your heart because you know Jesus? Will you have to cross Jordan alone? Why not drop on your knees now and let Jesus come into your heart as I pray.

Almighty God, giver and sustainer of life, I pray for the unsaved of this audience. May Thy Holy Spirit move upon their hearts and lives, right now, and save them by Thy power. In Thy name I pray. Amen.

41 — How Great Thou Art!

Once again this past week our attention has been focused on space with the astronauts landing on the moon. It is refreshing to know that many of the astronauts who have been involved in our space program have been men of faith in God. One of these astronauts is James B. Irwin. He was one of the first men to ride a dune buggy over the unexplored surface of the moon.

Recently, he testified of his faith in Jesus Christ. In Van Nuys, California he told large audiences that he had accepted Christ as his Savior at the age of eleven, and he also told how prayer had sustained him through all the trials before and during space training. As they orbited the globe and then started for the moon he said they could see Florida and the blue waters. And later they could see the continents, the whole earth in the beauty of color. He said the earth reminded them all of a very fragile Christmas tree ornament, surrounded by the blackness of space!

He told the audience that when he was on the moon, he was more conscious of God's presence, and felt closer to God than he had ever felt before. He would like to tell the whole world that God and Jesus Christ were there! And he added: "But most importantly, all of us thanked God for allowing us to leave the planet earth and explore our sister planet, the moon, and to return with new knowledge, new perspectives and new appreciation for spaceship earth."

As I read this testimony I thought of the wonderful insight into the omnipresence of God that it brought. The Psalmist, by faith must have had some such vision for he said, "Whither shall I go from Thy Spirit? Or whither shall I flee from Thy presence? If I ascend up into Heaven, thou art there: If I make my bed in Hell, behold thou art there. If I take the wings of the morning, and dwell in the uttermost parts of the sea; even there shall Thy hand lead me, and Thy right hand shall hold me."

When we consider how great God is in creating such a universe (of which the moon and the earth are but a small part) and of His dynamic presence everywhere we can understand how the things of the earth fall into their proper perspective! It makes us appreciate God's love to us who are such finite creatures in allowing His Son to come to die for our sins! We can only exclaim with the Psalmist: "How precious also are Thy thoughts unto me, O God! How great is the sum of them."

Ladies and gentlemen, the great God who made the heavens and the earth has provided for your salvation. Why not bow before Him right now and invite him into your heart?

Let us pray. Almighty God, Creator of the heavens and the earth, we enter Thy presence with thanksgiving at the opportunity of being intimate with the powerful King of the universe. We thank Thee for the provision of salvation through Thy Son Jesus Christ. I pray for those of this audience who are unsaved. May Thy Holy Spirit move upon their hearts and lives right now. In Thy name I pray. Amen!

42 — One Thing Lacking

The Bible records an incident in the life of our Lord when a very eager young man came running to Him. Kneeling before Him, he asked: "Good Master, what shall I do that I might inherit eternal life?" Jesus pointed to the Commandments: "Do not commit adultery, do not steal, do not kill, do not bear false witness, defraud not, and honour thy father and mother." The young man answered, "All these have I observed from my youth."

"Jesus, beholding him, loved him." Jesus was impressed by his humility, his hunger and his honorable life. It was His desire to help the man go all the way and accomplish his request, but the Lord was never known to offer a shortcut to salvation. He had no bargain to offer. Knowing that this man had a special love beside the desire for eternal life, He said, "One thing thou lackest: go thy way, sell whatsoever thou hast, and give to the poor, and thou shalt have treasures in heaven, and come take up thy cross and follow me."

"The young man was sad at that saying and went away grieved, for he had great possessions." This man had a desire for eternal life. He recognized the fact that Jesus was the giver of that life and he came to Him requesting it.

On the other hand, Jesus had a love for him and made known the means by which his request would be granted. But for the young man the price seemed too great. I believe that Jesus was sad by this young man's refusal. Saying to His disciples, "How hardly shall they that have riches enter into the kingdom of God because of their trust in riches." The disciples saw the interest of the rich young man, and they also recognized the love that Jesus showed for him. Seeing the desire for the salvation of this soul–yet the decision he made–the question arose in their minds, "Who then can be saved?"

He wanted salvation and the Lord wanted him to have it, but his desire for his present position overshadowed his desire to be saved, and in sorrow he walked away. Jesus likened the young man's efforts to a camel going through the eye of a needle. The disciples wondered if any could be saved and they became greatly concerned. Jesus seeing their troubled expression said, "With men it is impossible." By their natural ability alone it is impossible to pull themselves away from their sinful practices and keep themselves in the way they should go.

Many have tried again and again only to fail as many times as they tried. Many listening to me now have at one time or another realized your inability to help yourself as you faced the temptations of life. Jesus continues in His answer to the disciples' question that with God these things are possible. Many have been trying to free themselves without God. They find it impossible, but with God all the help that's needed will be supplied.

There is no case too hard for God. I am happy to tell you that I have seen many helpless people delivered from the clutches of alcoholism and similar vices, watching them repossess themselves in dignity and sobriety.

You may rest assured that your case is not hopeless. If your world is falling apart there is still hope. If society won't have you, if your friends have forsaken you, if business is frowning at you and your family is about to give you up as hopeless; there is still hope. You can be saved. God can lift you from the "guttermost" to the uttermost. Some of you have tried so hard until you are despairing that you can find yourself again, but don't despair. Christ is your answer.

In one minute's time you can find your freedom. When you come to Jesus and ask His forgiveness He performs a miracle of cleansing, but it's not beyond your reach for "With God all things are possible.

Ladies and gentlemen, there's room at the cross for you today. God can reach down right now and deliver from the power of sin.

Let us pray. Almighty God, giver and sustainer of life, I pray for those of this audience who are bound by the forces of sin and evil. Deliver them now. Let them feel Thy wonderful delivering touch upon their lives. Help them to reach the plateau in life that you created man for. I pray that you would put hope in the heart of those who are despairing. In Thy name I pray. Amen.

43 — Sin's Remedy

The power of Christ to save should not be minimized. The Bible says that "The Lord thy God in the midst of thee is mighty, and He will save."

When we look at man in his sinful condition we see a very dark picture. The Bible speaks of sinful man in Isaiah 1:5-6. These Scriptures state that the "Whole head is sick, and the whole heart is faint. From the sole of the foot even unto the head there is no soundness in it; but wounds, and bruises, and putrefying sores: they have not been closed, neither bound up, nor mollified with ointment."

As we look at the heart of man we become aware that no mere resolution, no turning over a new leaf, no simple act of joining the church, nor just trying to be a good citizen is sufficient to erase all of the sin of ones heart. Nothing short of the power of God, as revealed in the Gospel of our Lord Jesus Christ, can meet the need of the lost, sinful soul.

In this message I want to show you from the Bible that the power of Christ can save from the practice of sin. First, Christ can save from the practice of sin. The Bible admonishes in Isaiah 1:17 to cease to do evil and learn to do well. Again we read in Proverbs 28:13, "He that covereth his sins shall not prosper: But whoso confesseth them shall have mercy." Thus, to be saved from the practice of sin, one must look to Christ and His power to strengthen them to cease from that which defiles the soul.

Secondly, Christ saves from the guilt of sin. The Bible states in Romans 8:1–2 that "There is therefore now no condemnation to them which are in Christ Jesus, who walk not after the flesh, but after the spirit. For the law of the spirit of life in Christ Jesus hath made me free from the law of sin and death." What a wonderful feeling, to commit ones life to Christ and have the load of guilt and condemnation removed and to feel the wonderful freedom of salvation.

Thirdly, Christ saves from the power of sin. Romans 6:14 says, "Sin shall not have dominion over you." There are many today that were addicted to alcohol, dope, or other habits that now testify to complete deliverance by the power of God. I'm so thankful that Christ "breaks the power of cancelled sin and sets the prisoner free."

Is your life defiled by sin? Does the load of guilt and shame seem more than you can bear? Are you bound by the power of habits or dope? Then, I beg of you to turn to Christ with all of your heart. He alone can satisfy the need of your life. I ask you this morning to bow in the presence of Christ as I pray and invite Him into your heart and life.

Let us pray. Almighty God, I bow in Thy presence on behalf of those who are unsaved in this audience. Save from sin by Thy power. For those who are bound by the habits that are destroying their body and soul, deliver and set free by Thy great power. In Thy name I pray. Amen.

44 — Stormy Seas and Safe Havens

The other day I read the story of a whale named GIGI. GIGI was captured in Mexican waters shortly after her birth. She was brought to Sea World in San Diego, California, and placed in a small well-lighted tank. She was fed chopped squid and knew only humans and dolphins as companions. In one year she had grown to some seven tons and had become too big to remain in the tank.

It was decided to turn her loose into the ocean. But before doing this, scientists sewed a transmitter into her back that gives out radio signals. The navy had outfitted a fixed-winged aircraft to monitor her signal once or twice a week. Scientists had been driving up the coast with portable receiving gear to keep track of her.

To us, it may seem like a lot of effort and expense for a whale. But perhaps it is justifiable in the interest of science. Besides it is wonderful that they can keep track of the whale out in the mighty ocean.

In the Bible the oceans, or seas, are spoken of as representing the nations of the world in their restlessness and roaring. Isaiah 17:12 states, "Woe to the multitude of many people, which make a noise like the noise of the seas; and to the rushing of nations, that make a rushing like the rushing of mighty waters!"

The ocean water is salty and can never satisfy thirst! Each one of us is on this sea of life. What a joy it is to know that God is watching our every move and knows about us. And He doesn't need a transmitter either! He knows the restlessness of the wicked. For He says they are "Like the troubled sea, when it cannot rest, whose waters cast up mire and dirt." He knows the lack of satisfaction among the nations and He knows all about the tossing of the waves.

But He loves us. One day the Lord Jesus came into the nations of this earth and He went through the waves of sorrow and suffering for our sake. He could say, "All Thy waves and Thy billows are gone over me." If we will but cry to Him, He can bring us out of our distresses. He can make the storm a calm, so that the waves thereof are still. He can make us glad and one day bring us to the desired haven. "Then they cry unto the Lord in their trouble, and he bringeth them out of their distresses. He maketh the storm a calm, so that the waves thereof are still. Then are they glad because they be quiet; so he bringeth them unto their desired haven. Oh that men would praise the Lord for his goodness, and for His wonderful works to the children of men!" (Psalm 107:28-31).

Are you tossed in a life with no way out? Then, I ask you to turn to Christ as we pray. He will hear your cry and meet your need.

Let us pray. Almighty God, I thank you that in times of distress, perplexity, and despondency we can call on your name with the confidence that you hear us when we pray. I pray for those of this audience who are seemingly lost at sea. May they feel the wonderful arms of Jesus surround them at this moment and may they be lifted from despairing waters. In Thy name I pray. Amen!

45 — It's Time to Get Up!

A few days ago I read the story of a little boy who was walking along with his mother, all dressed up for a special party. As is characteristic of little boys, full of life and energy, he was romping around, hopscotching here and there. His mother warned him, "Be careful, calm down, you're going to fall down and get all messed up." The boy absorbed by his interest in his fun kept on, and as you would expect, he did fall down and was covered with mud. His mother stopped, looked at him, squared herself with hands on her hips and with an accusing voice asked, "Now, what are you going to do?" With amazing composure in such a situation, he simply replied, "I'm going to get up."

When I read this story, the moral of it came through loud and clear. Who hasn't found himself in a similar situation in the "rough and tumble" of life. However, we should not settle for a way of life that is always on a familiar and comfortable path; but rather, there should be some daring adventure on our part so we can break away from the common patterns of life.

The secret of success that characterized the little boy of our story was the ability to recognize the first step of recovery. He simply said, "I'm going to get up." Nothing is accomplished, if after a tumble in life, we remain in that position while trying to determine all the steps required for recovery. A good football player, when realizing that a fall is finally inevitable, falls forward, determined to gain every foot possible even when falling. In addition to that he arises at the first possible instant, continues in the game leaving the "fall" behind.

Life is full of examples of those who have 'fallen in the mud' who lie there contemplating all the moves of the future. That's not a very inspiring position from which to make decisions. And very often they remain there. However, it is better to get up and get going.

The Bible teaches that the apostle Paul understood this principle for he said, "Forgetting those things that are behind I press on toward the mark." His goal was before him. The scripture teaches of man that as he "thinketh in his heart so is he." Since that is true should we not claim the promise? For God said His peace shall be a garrison to our hearts and minds. That we may be guarded from not only those easily identified base and evil thoughts, but from thoughts that are lesser than those which God would have us think. God's thoughts would instead lead us on to contributions to our generation consistent with God's purposes for us.

Therefore, I ask, "Have you stumbled and fallen in the mud?" Then, get up and get going by the power of God. Determine from this day forward to make your life count for God and good. With God's help you can do it. I ask you to bow in the presence of Christ as we entreat His divine help in moving forward in life.

Let us pray. Almighty God, giver and sustainer of life, we bow in Thy presence asking for Thy divine strength and help for those who have fallen along the way. Help them to arise and go forward in the name of the Lord. In Thy name I pray. Amen.

46 — Rebellion

Rebellion is engulfing the world. We find it in the remote areas of the world and on the wide-lighted thoroughfares of America. We see rebellion on the college campuses and in the Church.

Rebellion is the spirit of the age! This is in keeping with man's history. The first rebellion occurred when Lucifer, the most beautiful angel in Heaven, challenged God's authority. This rebellion will culminate in the final drama of the ages, when the antichrist and his armies shall be crushed forever by our all-conquering King!

The final rebellion is building in the world now. John said, "The spirit of the antichrist...even now already is it in the world." And it seems that this rebellion gathers momentum every day. Rebellion against moral and civil laws makes the biggest headlines today. But rebellion against spiritual laws is the most serious and is at the root of all other rebellion.

This age has seen a theological revolt against sound doctrine, such as denying the virgin birth of Christ, denying the authority of the Scriptures, the person of the Holy Spirit and the authenticity of the resurrection. This revolt has not only come from the outside of the Church, but by leaders within an apostate Church. We need to be aware of the thin line between seeking answers and questioning God. And this generation is moving from a questioning stance to an obstinate stance where statements against the Church and its leaders are commonplace.

Thus, we question, "What is God's attitude toward rebellion?" Samuel told King Saul: "Rebellion is as the sin of witchcraft." And God said, "Thou shalt not suffer a witch to live." God has promised swift destruction in the last rebellion of time. Through faith in Christ, God offers man an alternative to rebellion. His alternative sounds paradoxical, but it works. He says, "Surrender and win, lose and gain, yield to be victorious." His word teaches strength through submission. That's the alternative, instead of rebellion, submission to God's perfect will.

The most successful lifestyles are of people who have learned the secrets of Romans 12:1. "I beseech you therefore, brethren by the mercies of God, that ye present your bodies a living sacrifice, holy, acceptable unto God, which is your reasonable service."

Consider the contrast between King Saul who rebelled and died in infamy and the Saul who surrendered to God to live and die a hero, as the apostle Paul. Or look at the example of our Lord in Gethsemane as He surrendered with "Not my will, but thine be done."

In the year 1803 it seemed that every student at Yale University was an infidel. There was a rebellion against religion, with many students assuming names of French and English atheists. Adoniram Judson was a student there, and a rebellious one. One day a chaplain approached Judson with the suggestion that he become a minister. Young Judson replied, "How could a skeptic like me enter into such trivial things? I'll ride north and let the wind of faith decide my career."

This rebellious youth rode his horse out of town and spent the night at an inn. A student leader, an avowed atheist and Judson's hero spent the night in an adjoining room. A sudden attack of pneumonia took the life of the young atheist that night. Through the thin walls of the inn Judson could hear him crying to God for mercy as he felt the flames of hell about him. There in a lonely inn the skeptic Judson knelt beside his bed and surrendered to God. He brought him to Burma later as a missionary. A life destined to shipwreck was changed to one of history's greats, by one step: the step to surrender.

If you are attracted by the rebellion of this age look carefully at where it leads and take the alternative. Resist the wickedness of our time and give yourself to God for submission to Him is that alternative.

Let us pray. Almighty God, I enter Thy presence on behalf of this audience who have resisted and rebelled against Thy ways. May Thy Holy Spirit arrest them in this hour and make them aware that the only way to peace, happiness and life everlasting is by surrendering to the Lord Jesus Christ. In Thy name I pray. Amen.

•

47 — The Right Start

This week at our church we will be placing special emphasis on reaching boys and girls with the gospel of Jesus Christ. With this fact in mind I would like to address my remarks to the subject of "The Right Start in Life."

We look into the Holy Scriptures and take note of the life of our Lord. The Scriptures do not have much to say concerning the earthy childhood of Christ; however, there is this comment that "the child grew and waxed strong in spirit filled with wisdom; and the grace of God was upon him." Here is a condensed commentary upon His physical, mental, and spiritual growth. In addition to these natural developments, the grace of God is mentioned as resting upon Him. Thus we note that He was a natural human boy, developing in the ordinary fashion and accompanied by the presence and grace of His Father.

From the age of twelve until He was thirty, the Bible is completely silent concerning Christ's life. The only comment on His life during these eighteen years was that "Jesus increased in wisdom and stature, and in favor with God and man." Thus, we conclude that in the years before He was 12 he had grown and become filled with wisdom. And now after twelve and on into maturity, He still increased in wisdom and stature.

As we look into the life of Christ we become aware of certain basic things that had a bearing and impact upon His life. These things are essential for the right start in life. First, let us look at His parents. They were a godly couple. The Bible says concerning Mary, "Thou art highly favoured, the Lord is with thee...blessed art thou among women...." And concerning Joseph the Scriptures declare he was "a just man." This means that he walked uprightly before God and was a man subject to God. I believe it is necessary and essential for parents to set a godly example before their children. Parents in this 20th century need to wake up and use their influence to save this generation.

We need more Godly parents concerned about the spiritual life of their children.

The second thing we note about Christ is His education. We are told that the formal education of Jesus began when He was six years of age as He followed the Jewish custom of attending the local school of the Rabbis. Thus, His education was based on and permeated by knowledge of the Old Testament Law.

There is a great truth here for us because the education of Christ had taken deep roots in His life, in that it started young. These first years are so important as children need guidance. They need examples and teachings about God. Some parents might say, "I do not believe in influencing children in the decisions they make relating to religion." But Ladies and gentlemen, if you do not influence them, the public schools will, the newspapers will, the comics will, the TV and radio will, their companions and the communists will.

It is essential that children be taught the high standard of Christian values. They must be taught to distinguish between right and wrong so that they may make the right decisions. As parents, we must do all in our power to develop and protect their spiritual life.

The Bible says, "Train up a child in the way he should go; and when he is old, he will not depart from it." The word train in this scripture needs emphasis. It means to direct the growth of, to form by instruction or to make prepared for a test. This is the parents responsibility; however, there are so many who leave the spiritual welfare of their children to the pastor or the Sunday school teacher.

I beg of you parents listening to this broadcast today, don't leave to the pastor and Sunday school teacher to do on Sunday morning what you should be doing all week. The end result will be a child brought up in the nurture and admonition of the Lord and they will be prepared to stand against life's trials and tests.

Let us pray. Almighty God, giver and sustainer of life, I pray for every parent listening to this program today. May the great obligation of parenthood grip their lives as never before. Help them to know the opportunities of training a soul for eternity. In Thy name I pray. Amen.

48 — The ABCs of the Gospel

As speaker on the "Christ in the Now" radio broadcast, I have a strong desire to bring to you the simplicity of the gospel of Jesus Christ. Today, I want to bring to you the ABCs of the gospel. If you will follow the instructions of this message you can become a Christian. I want you to know it isn't hard to come to God. In fact, it's easy because Jesus did the work on Calvary, and it's up to you to accept His efforts for yourself.

First, the Bible says in Romans 3:23, "All have sinned, and come short of the glory of God." This fact must be realized and accepted or else we could not see any reason for personal repentance. Everyone you know and are associated with comes under this fact of sin.

The evil tendencies of this life are born out of the spiritual blood poison passed on to us by Adam and Eve when they made a deal with the serpent in the Garden. By their transgression, sin was passed upon the entire population of the world and every generation.

Secondly, the Bible says, "Behold, what manner of love the Father hath bestowed upon us that we should be called the sons of God." Mankind, the highest hope of God, is the apple of His eye. Man had insulted God, ignored Him and walked away giving heed to the temptation of the devil. Human love might become exhausted and give up in such a case but God's love made Him work to gain man back to Himself. His love was active, working, reaching, and sacrificing all for the benefit of man to bring him back into association with God.

It was not the strength of the soldiers that held Jesus in the judgement; neither the spikes that held Him to the cross, but it was a love stronger than the sting of the whip and the struggle of death. The world's greatest portrayal of love will be seen as you behold Jesus on the cross with the spittle still on His face, and the blood running over His face from the thorn crowned brow. As He sees His heartbroken mother standing in agony and despair amid the scoffers He cries out, "Father forgive them for they know not what they do." My friends, the strength of God's love reaches beneath the lowest and above the highest and around us all and no one can escape His love.

Thirdly, Jesus says, "Come unto me all ye that labour and are heavy laden and I will give you rest." What an invitation! It takes in every burden, every problem, every guilt and every stain. Jesus is the only one who can give such an invitation to such a needy world. You may try to get away from your hard-pressed feeling and you may attempt to lay your burden down by your own efforts; but, there still remains that restless, anxious feeling and your conscience will continue to prick you until Jesus gives you rest.

I ask you today, why be miserable when you can be happy? Why be sad when you can be glad? Why be bound when you can be free?

The blood of Jesus Christ has made it possible for you to have an easy way out. The price has been paid for your ransom, and if you will come to Jesus, the things you are laboring with will vanish and the heavy load you carry will disappear.

In 30 seconds I will give you three easy steps by which you can find God. In these few seconds, why not bow before the Lord and invite Him into your heart.

My friends, I give you three steps to God. The first step to forgiveness is found in Isaiah 55:7, which says, "Let the wicked forsake his way and the unrighteous man his thoughts, and let him return unto the Lord and he will have mercy upon him: and to our God, for he will abundantly pardon." Quit the things that are wrong, turn from the evil practices and tell the devil you are through with him. You can make up your mind right now that you are through with your evil ways. It doesn't take a week, month, or a year to quit, just quit now and you have made the first step toward God.

The second step to God is found in I John 1:9 which says, "If we confess our sins, he is faithful and just to forgive us our sins, and to cleanse us from all unrighteousness." After we quit our wrong and make a trash pile of our guilt, it is only logical that we tell God we are sorry for our wrong. We plead guilty before God and when this confession is made, God forgives.

The third step to God is found in Romans 5:1 that tells us, "Therefore being justified by faith we have peace with God through our Lord Jesus Christ." When you have forsaken your sins and have confessed them unto God there is no reason why you should question that God has done His part. It is this trusting faith that gives us peace with God. Lean back in the arms of Jesus and be assured that you are forgiven when you have forsaken sin and confessed your sin and now believe God to be your forgiver and Savior.

Let us pray. Lord Jesus, I pray for everyone who is bowing in Thy presence right now. Give them power to turn from sin and place their faith and trust in You. In Thy name I pray. Amen.

49 — Free at Last

On July the 4th, 1776, the Continental Congress adopted the Declaration of Independence. It was a declaration declaring the American colonies free from Europe. This was a great day in the history of our nation and it is right that we celebrate this event.

The last sentence of this declaration states, "And for the support of this declaration, with a firm reliance of the protection of Divine Providence, we mutually pledge to each other our lives, our fortunes, and our sacred honor."

These men recognized the need of God to make our nation great. They knew that God's power would have to be the protection of a young, small and struggling state. Therefore, they expressed a "firm reliance on the protection of Divine Providence."

But this morning, I would like to turn our attention to another kind of freedom and that is the inner freedom of man. Man searches for freedom in a thousand ways. However, there would be no need for such a struggle if man could bring himself to accept and use the freedom God offers to everyone. When God sets our goals and supplies the criteria for our judgements and our interests, we are in the free place where He intends us to live. And when this happens, the creative limits of God become the limits of our souls, minds, and spirits.

Man, from the very beginning, has contrived to bind himself. Our first parents thought they were grabbing liberation when actually they grabbed bondage. And until God sent His Son, Jesus Christ, to announce release to the captives, no one was free.

God sent His Son to clarify Himself to man because His Son was free to remain His wholly divine self. This He was able to do in the midst of the hatred, cruelty and viciousness of man's world. Through every day of His life on earth, Jesus Christ lived freedom. When we realize this, we become aware that if Jesus makes a man free, that man is free indeed.

Emancipation from bondage means the door is wide open to more and more of life. It leads to peace, joy, satisfaction and happiness.

We do not receive this freedom by following rigid lines of rules and legalism, we receive it by following Christ. When the self-righteous Pharisees took up stones to kill the woman caught in the act of adultery, Jesus said, "Let him who is without sin among you be the first to throw a stone at her." These Pharisees followed certain rules and became so proud that their hearts were twisted out of shape, their capacities to love and to care became cramped and bound; and what they thought was freedom actually became bondage.

Jesus did not step according to their rules and they crucified him, but this did not rid them of His caring. Jesus came forth from the tomb and started towards the human race, and at this moment He is walking toward you with inner freedom. Freedom is not something we find; it is something God gives. And at this very moment He wants to put His freedom in your heart.

As we pray, I ask you to totally commit your life to Christ. Let Him break the bondage and yoke that binds, so that on this July 4th you can truly know what freedom means.

Let us pray. Almighty God, liberate those who are bound by sin. Set them free by Thy power. Liberate those who are bound by sickness and disease. Let them feel Thy wonderful touch. Set the captives free. In Thy name I pray. Amen.

50 — Holiday or Holy Day?

At this sacred season of the year, the world comes under the magical spell of Christmas. There is a light of hope and expectation in the eyes of the children. The bright holiday decorations are brought from their places of storage, and once again they deck the happy halls of our homes. The air is filled with the sound of caroling, and a happy twinkle is found in the misty eyes of both young and old.

Something happens at Christmas to change the normal routine of life. There is a new zest, a keen anticipation and a gracious spirit of sharing that permeates the atmosphere. The truth of God's love to mankind is proclaimed that "God so loved the world that He gave His only begotten Son that whosoever believeth in Him should not perish but have everlasting life."

I ask you today what does Christmas really mean to you? To some, it is just a holiday. To others, it is just a time to promote their business. But to the Christian, it has an entirely different meaning.

The real meaning of Christmas can be realized in your life. This can be the merriest Christmas you have ever had if you will kneel in the presence of the eternal Christ and ask Him to come into your heart.

Let us pray. Almighty God, we bow in the presence of the Christ who came to earth to redeem fallen mankind. I pray for those at this Christmas season that do not know the Christ who came to redeem them. Help them to realize that the greatest gift they can receive at this Christmas season is the gift of God and eternal life–Jesus Christ–in their heart. In Thy name I pray. Amen.

51 — What is Christ Doing Now?

The work of Christ in the hearts of men did not cease when He returned to Heaven. The work of salvation, healing, and comforting is still being carried on. Christ is still the "one who sticks closer than a brother." He is still the "Lily of the valley and the bright and the morning star." He is still the one who said, "I will never leave thee nor forsake thee, but will be with you always, even unto the end of the world."

Hebrews 7:25 affirms that Christ is "able to save them to the uttermost that come unto God by him, seeing he ever liveth to make intercession for them." Again in Hebrews 13:8 we note that "Jesus Christ is the same yesterday, today and forever." His power has never diminished. His love and compassion still knows no bounds. Ladies and gentlemen, He is definitely concerned about every need of your life. There are three things from Hebrews 7:25 that I want to bring to your attention in this message.

First, Christ is able to save completely all that come to God through Him. The emphasis here is on God's power and the depths from which that power can lift. There is no depth of iniquity to which man can descend from which the power of Christ cannot lift. His salvation extends to the worst. Such is the greatness of Christ's sympathy and power that He reaches down to the lowest and lifts them to the heights of purity and glory. There are no crimes against Heaven and earth that the mercy of God in Jesus Christ will not cover. If you want to be saved today, you must approach God on the basis of Christ's saviorhood as revealed in both His person and His work on the Cross.

Secondly, the scripture states that "He ever liveth." Again the Bible declares that Christ "continueth forever and hath an unchangeable priesthood." There were many priests under the Old Covenant and they all died. But Jesus, the great High Priest is alive forever more. Many systems have had a brief day of power and have passed away. Then the testing time came and they have waned and disappeared. But Jesus Christ has not lost one jot or tittle of His power to save and heal.

Thirdly, this scripture notes that the reason "He ever liveth" is to "make intercession." Thus, He is the perpetual intercessor. His presentation of the believer at the throne of God, made possible by His resurrection, argues for the undiminished adequacy of His ability to effect a perfect salvation. The Bible says in I John 2:1, "We have an advocate with the Father, Jesus Christ the righteous." Hebrews 9:24 states, "For Christ is not entered into the Holy Place made with hands, which are the figures of the true; but into Heaven itself, now to appear in the presence of God for us."

Ladies and gentlemen, this very moment you can come to God through Jesus Christ. He is waiting to intercede for you. I ask you to bow in His eternal presence and invite Him into your heart as I pray.

Almighty God, the One who gave His "only begotten Son" to die on the cross for our sins, we enter Thy eternal and holy presence thanking Thee for the provision of salvation. I pray for those of this audience who are not saved. May they know the joys of salvation at this very moment. May they feel the presence of the resurrected Christ in a very definite way. I pray for those who need Thy healing touch upon their lives. Heal them now and make them whole by Thy great and wonderful power. In Thy name I pray. Amen.

52 — It's Not an Easy Road

In His Great High Priestly prayer to His Father, Jesus asked many things for His disciples, but one request He would not make. It is recorded in John 17:15 that Jesus prayed, "I pray not that thou shouldest keep them from the evil." From this scripture we are aware that the world is the believer's battleground and here he must win or lose.

We sometimes encounter people who use their environment as an excuse for failure as a Christian. A teenage girl said to me one time, "I'd like to be a Christian. I know it is the only way to live, but none of my friends at school are Christians. I could never serve God in that setup!"

However, as I look into the Scriptures I note that the New Testament scarcely considers surroundings a handicap for believers. The early disciples were never promised pampering, it was going to be a rough way, if they gave themselves to the Master. Jesus used grim language to warn them how hard the road would be. He talked of cutting off feet and hands, of plucking out eyes, of squeezing through tight gates and walking in narrow paths, of forsaking friends and property, and of counting one's life expendable for His sake.

One searches in vain through the Book of Acts for a hint of softness among the believers. None of them asked if they should leave their particular community to escape persecution. They expected persecution; they invaded communities where they knew fearful opposition awaited them. They were not out to escape the world, but to change it–and they did. There were saints in Caesar's household. There were men of whom their enemies said they "turned the world upside down."

The story is told of a bishop visiting an African country and was confronted by a hungry national who asked for 50 cents. The bishop gave him the money. The man clenched it tightly in his hand and said, "I am hungry, but I am not going to use this money for food. I am going to put it toward the cost of getting out our propaganda paper for communism. For I am a communist, sir, and it will require great sacrifice for us to save the world from imperialism!" When the bishop returned to America, he said sadly to his people that if Christians were as committed to Christ as that African was to Marxism, he would have cause for great rejoicing.

One Christian leader has said, "We Christians are losing the world with the Truth. The communists are winning it with a lie!" It is high time for us who believe to examine our hearts and minds and ask why men who promote error are more dedicated to their tasks than those who have the Word of God.

Jesus called His disciples "the light of the world." Other lights have little to do when the sun blazes down at noon! Turn on the headlamps of your automobile at 2 p.m. on a cloudless day and you will note that nothing seems to happen. But switch them on at midnight and see how bright they are. Ladies and gentlemen, the Church was not built in the Garden of Eden; it was built in the wastelands of sin. It does not blossom in a flowery park but in a thorny wilderness. God expects Christians to "let their light shine that others might know the joys of salvation." Don't run away when the going gets hard. Our problems are not geographical; they are moral and spiritual. Committed Christians are a stubborn lot. They do not crack up easily. Their sign is not a couch, but a cross. The believer who cannot in some measure change his world will himself be changed by the world. We are not here to outrun the world, but to overcome it. The Bible says, "For whatsoever is born of God overcometh the world, even our faith."

Let us pray. Almighty God, I pray for every believer in this community. Give them power to live dedicated, overcoming lives for Thee. In Thy name I pray. Amen.

53 — Two Baptisms, Two Baptizers

John the Baptist was clearly referring to the Lord Jesus Christ when he said, "I indeed have baptized you with water: but he shall baptize you with the Holy Ghost" (Mark 1:8). This statement refers to two baptisms and two baptizers. And the two are placed in contrast to each other.

The best way to teach people about something they have never seen is to start with that which is familiar to them. For example, according to Luke 11:13, Jesus said, "If ye then, being evil, know how to give good gifts unto your children: how much more shall your heavenly Father give the Holy Spirit to them that ask him?" We know what earthly fathers are like and if we know how an earthly father loves to give good gifts to his children, we can imagine how much our heavenly Father delights in giving the Holy Spirit to those who ask Him. Thus, we learn about the heavenly Father from what we know about earthly fathers. We learn about the baptism in the Holy Spirit from what we know about water baptism.

So, let us look at the two baptisms. John did his baptizing in the river Jordan because there was enough water there to immerse the people. I am a confirmed believer in baptism by immersion. There are three things about baptism in water I want to bring to your attention. First, it is something you can feel. Secondly, it is something that is evident to the people who are watching. And thirdly, it is a definite experience. The baptized person knows when and where it happened. No one can be baptized and be unaware that he is going under the water.

So we learn that the baptism in the Spirit is something one can feel. It is something that others can see and the person himself knows it has happened to him. The Bible records instances of various people receiving the baptism in the Spirit, in order that we might compare our experience with theirs. We find it happened exactly as John indicated. It was felt. It was evident to others and it was a definite experience. We read in Acts 8:18 that Simon saw that through laying on of the apostles' hands the Holy Ghost was given. How could he have seen this if there had not been definite evidence?

Then we read in Acts 10:44, "while Peter yet spake these words, the Holy Ghost fell on all them which heard the word." Later on, when reporting this event to the believers at Jerusalem, Peter said, "And as I began to speak, the Holy Ghost fell on them, as on us at the beginning." He identified this with the baptism in the Holy Spirit that he and others had received on the Day of Pentecost. John wanted everyone to know that the baptism in the Spirit would be felt just as much as when he baptized them in Jordan. When John baptized them, persons came up dripping. And when Jesus baptizes persons in the Spirit they come up saturated with the Spirit. Those nearby will hear them speak in tongues.

Now let us look at the two baptizers of these two baptisms. John said, "I indeed have baptized you with water: but he shall baptize you with the Holy Ghost." John was a man and when you go to a man of God to request baptism, he will ask whether you have repented of your sins and have placed your faith in Christ. And when you come to Jesus to be baptized with the Holy Spirit, you have to meet certain conditions. These are spelled out in Acts 2:38 where Peter said: "Repent, and be baptized every one of you in the name of Jesus Christ for the remission of sins, and ye shall receive the gift of the Holy Ghost."

Ladies and gentlemen, are you repentant? Do you hate sin? Do you have faith in the cleansing blood of Jesus? If your heart is cleansed, and if it is a repentant, humble and believing heart, you can come to Jesus and receive this baptism. You do not come to a mere man for this baptism, but to the Lord. Men cannot baptize you in the Holy Spirit; only Jesus can do that. What you must do is exactly the same as when you went to the minister to be baptized in water. You must put yourself entirely in the hands of the Baptizer, the Lord Jesus.

Let us pray. Almighty God, I pray for those of Thy children, who have not been baptized in the Holy Spirit that right now they shall know the wonderful experience of being immersed in Thy Holy Spirit. In Thy name I pray. Amen.

54 — Chills or Thrills?

A Victorian idea seems to have established itself in this generation, and unfortunately it is still spreading. It claims that being a Christian makes you dull and a killjoy. It claims that when you commit your life to Christ, your world comes to an end and you no longer enjoy living. A related idea popular among certain people is that only squares go to church. They claim the real life is outside religion or, at least, outside organized religion.

In this message I would like to dispute both ideas. I believe that when a person finds Christ as Savior, then he really begins to live. A horizon opens to him of which the human mind could never even dream. This thrill can be yours only when Jesus Christ is complete Lord and Master of your life. Jesus Christ came into the world to bring light and liberty, to destroy the works of Satan, and to regain all that was lost to Satan's dominion. This is why any experience less than the overpowering thrill of belonging to Christ will bring only disappointment to you and discredit to the cause of Christ. There are at least six different thrills that will come to you when you belong to Christ.

The first is the reality of having and possessing the peace of God. Others may talk about peace. They may desire it, even strive for it; but, as a Christian you possess it. It is a tranquillity that is simply glorious.

The second thrill is the blessing of the complete inward knowledge of sins forgiven. This understanding, born of God's Spirit, reveals to you that every sin committed since the day of responsibility is now forgiven. It reveals that in the sight of God you stand as though you had never sinned and you are no longer guilty. This knowledge comes through your mind and intellect, as you understand the Scriptures. It also comes through your heart as God's Spirit bears witness with your human spirit.

The third thrill is the abolition of fear. All fear disappears, and in its place comes a quiet serenity that surely is divine. All the previous frustrations, anxieties, and irritations have now vanished. They have been removed by the power of God as you love Him and come into His fellowship.

The fourth thrill is hope, born of an assurance that will ever remain with you. This is the hope of security of your future destiny, the hope and joy of seeing loved ones again, and the blessed hope of one day seeing Jesus Christ.

The fifth thrill is the feeling that you belong, that you are wanted. All Christians are set and planted in the Church and made an integral part of His body. Your name is recorded in the Lamb's Book of Life. Your human body becomes the dwelling place of God's Holy Spirit, and you are now a working partner with God. Loneliness is forever banished, for you can talk to God any moment of the day or night.

The sixth thrill is knowing that you are incorporated into a great plan. The Master Potter will now mold and shape your life into usefulness and beauty. Although you still retain your individuality and your own personality, you become part of a vast whole. You are not your own, you now belong to Jesus Christ. You are sustained by His life and all your future security is in His hands. Consequently there is no torment, no fear, no isolation. There are no sins, no frustrations, and no darknesses, for you are kept by the power of God. All this is but a fragment of the ever-increasing thrill that comes to the person who hands his life over unconditionally to Jesus Christ. There is no other way, no other plan, only deep sincere sorrow for your sins, forsaking your sins, trusting implicitly in the work of Jesus Christ and His death on the cross.

Let us pray. Almighty God, giver and sustainer of life, I pray for those who have heard this sermon who do not know Thy joy and presence. Let them feel the nearness of the Son of God and may they experience these wonderful thrills of salvation. In Thy name I pray. Amen.

55 — A Resolute Love

In the 24th chapter of the book of Genesis, a very beautiful love story is recorded. The key words of this story are, "I will go." In this story, Abraham had conceived the plan of sending a servant to the old country to find a bride for his son Isaac. The servant, whose name was Eliezer, faithfully carried out his part of the plan by going to the right place and speaking the right words. His job could scarcely have been done with better efficiency and grace. In the tents of Abraham the prospective bridegroom waited, prayed, watched the horizon and momentarily expected the return of the servant.

This Old Testament Bible story is a beautiful picture of the great plan of salvation. At the present time, the heavenly Servant, the Holy Spirit, is here on His divine errand of finding a bride for Christ. The bridegroom is spending His time in the heavenly tabernacle, waiting, praying and looking forward to the return of the Holy Spirit with the bride.

When an individual is asked by the Holy Spirit to leave the old pattern of life to start a new life, it is often a time of tremendous tension and soul searching. This decision took C.T. Studd from the English cricket fields to the Orient. For David Livingston it meant going through Africa's steaming jungles. Daniel's decision led through a lion's den and a king's banquet hall. The decision to go led Paul from the Damascus Road to the block of a Roman executioner. And when we consider where these men were led, we question what is the compelling force that has led millions to make this journey? What is it about God's plan of redemption that causes men to take up the cross, reverse their present order of life, and follow the Holy Spirit into the unknown future?

Among the reasons for this we must consider first the work of the Holy Spirit. With each one of our hearts He has used the utmost tact, courtesy, and earnestness in persuading us to make the journey to Heaven. He has faithfully carried out His mission of telling us about the Lord, and has not exalted Himself or sought any personnel praise. His sole purpose has been to carry out the plan of the Father. And He has pledged to see us safely through if we will go with Him.

Another reason individuals decide to go is the enjoyment of the gifts and graces the Lord has sent as tokens of His love. We may enjoy these gifts while the journey progresses. Isaac had sent much jewelry and other beautiful things to Rebecca. Acceptance of these indicated her response to his love. Similarly, Jesus has instructed the Holy Spirit to adorn the bride with spiritual gifts, graces of character, fruits of righteousness, and all that is needed to prepare her for the mighty events at the end of the journey.

Finally, it is wise to remember in this love story that evening finally came. The Bible says, "Isaac went out to meditate in the fields at the eventide: and he lifted up his eyes, and saw, and behold, the camels were coming." The years are passing rapidly and every sign indicates that we are approaching the journey's end. We will soon be at the tents of our heavenly Isaac. Jesus said, "I will come again and receive you unto myself, that where I am there shall ye be also." But we must remember this: the decision to go with the Holy Spirit is always a personal decision. No one can decide for another, and no one ever regretted making his decision for God. Someone has said, "The road behind was rugged and the road ahead seems long...But it leads at last to life's eternal goal: So I'll keep on pressing forward with a smile and with a song–For just o'er the next horizon I'll see Jesus."

Ladies and gentlemen, at this moment the Holy Spirit speaks and I invite you to accept His invitation as we pray.

Almighty God, I bow in Thy presence, asking that Thy Holy Spirit would make real the wonderful invitation of the heavenly bridegroom, Jesus Christ. Help each one who has heard this message make the right decision in regards to salvation. In Thy name I pray. Amen.

56 — The Sacrificial Lamb

In the 22nd chapter of the book of Genesis we have recorded a conversation between Abraham and his son Isaac. The setting for this conversation is that Abraham is climbing the mountain on which he is to offer his son as a sacrifice in obedience to the command of the Lord. As they traverse to the top of the mountain Isaac asks his Father, "Where is the Lamb" to which the Father answers, "My Son, God will provide Himself a lamb."

During this climb up the top of the mountain all the gamut of human emotions must have raced through the soul of Abraham and Isaac. Abraham was determined to obey the will of God and Isaac surrendered to the will of his father. There must have been temptations for each not to go through with the ordeal. Then finally the peak is reached in human emotions in the final moments of this drama as Abraham prepares to completely obey God. Then suddenly God becomes Jehovah-Jireh and a lamb is provided. As we look into the Scriptures we note that in the crisis times of human history, God has always provided a lamb.

We first note this in the land of Egypt when the children of Israel sighed by reason of the bondage as they cried and groaned. No doubt they cried, "Is there not a God who will answer and meet our need?" Then the Bible teaches that God heard their groaning and remembered their covenants and He provided a lamb whereby they were delivered from the land of Egypt.

The second time we see God sending a lamb was in more affluent times when the children of Israel were safe in their own land. Worship and service had eroded to pomp ceremony, the Sadducees split hairs over the resurrection of the body, and the Pharisees were making much to do about mint and cumin. At this time the sincere and spiritually famished must have cried, "Is there not a God of reality?" And God sent His only begotten Son, and John the Baptist said, "Behold, the Lamb of God which taketh away the sins of the world." Thus, to a nation dead in ceremony and ritual, God provided a Lamb.

Then, we turn to the fifth chapter of Revelation and we find the description of a universe in chaos, war, and complete frustration. Vials are being poured out, seals are being broken, the books are being opened and judgements are being administered. Man's inheritance is lost, and in despair John weeps.

Then one of the elders tells John to dry his tears and weep no more, for he has found One who is worthy to break the seals and redeem the lost inheritance. And when John looked, he saw a "Lamb as it had been slain." Thus to a world in chaos, rebellion, and fear God provided a Lamb.

Today, we might question, "Where is the Lamb to meet the needs of frustrated humanity?" The Scriptures teach that He is sitting at the right hand of the Father making intercession for you. In your gravest and most terrible hour, when your heart breaks and your soul cries out, "Oh God, where is the Lamb?" God answers, "He is here right beside me making intercession for you." God is still revealing Himself as Jehovah-Jireh. He is still providing a Lamb!

Ladies and gentlemen, whatever needs you may have in your life, the Lamb of God waits to intercede on your behalf. He is the high priest that is touched by the feeling of your infirmities. I ask you to bow in His eternal presence as I pray.

Almighty God, the One who has always and doth even today provide a Lamb for His people, I enter Thy presence now on behalf of those of this audience who are burdened with the cares and anxieties of this life. May they know the delivering power of God in a great and wonderful way. In Thy name I pray. Amen.

57 — Anniversary Broadcast

On this anniversary broadcast of "Christ in the Now" I would like to reinstate the purpose of this ministry. Contrary to what many think, God is alive today, doing His work of redemption, changing the lives of men and women, giving hope, health and assurance in an age of anxiety. And the message of this broadcast presents a living God whose power has not diminished with the passing of time. He is the God of Abraham, Isaac, and Jacob. He is the God who has revealed Himself through His Word, the Holy Bible, and who has spoken to us through His Son, Jesus Christ.

First, we present the Christ who saves. The Bible tells us that Christ saves to the uttermost, and if you will believe on Him, He can save you from the penalty of sin. He can save you from the crisis of sin's hold in your life. He can save you from your worries and fears. He can change your life and transform you from a sinner to a saint. He can give you a purpose for life and an inner strength to meet every problem.

Second, we present a Christ who heals. Only Christ can see you as a total person–body, soul, and spirit. His compassion extends to your physical body, even as He is able to see the needs of your soul and spirit. The Bible says, "He is the same yesterday, today and forever." His power has not been diminished. He can heal today.

Third, we present a Christ who empowers for service. He has promised to fill you with His Holy Spirit. The Bible says, "Ye shall receive power after that the Holy Ghost is come upon you, and ye shall be witnesses unto me." The Holy Spirit will not only abide with you and instruct, but He will provide you power for bringing the unsaved to Christ so that your witness will not depend upon "lofty words of wisdom...but in demonstration of the Spirit and Power."

The fourth purpose of this radio ministry is to present a Christ who is coming again. He will come to take those who have faith in Him, and "so shall we ever be with the Lord."

When Christ comes again, He will come to judge. First of all, he will judge every believer. He will not judge to condemn but rather their works, so He can reward for their faithfulness. Then, He will judge the world. On that day, everything that is hidden will be revealed, and sin will be unmasked for what it is. Hypocrites will have no place to hide. The tares will be separated from the wheat, the sheep from the goats and wolves will be stripped of their sheep's clothing. But those who have cast their allegiance to Jesus Christ will have no fear on that last day of crisis. The Bible says, "Little children, abide in Him, so that when He appears we may have confidence and not shrink from Him in shame at His coming."

Life has many crises and only a complete confidence in Jesus Christ will help you overcome every one of them.

It is our prayer as you listen to this broadcast that you will meet Christ. And believing in Him you will find the answer for the crisis you may now be facing.

Let us pray. Almighty God, giver and sustainer of life, we bow in Thy presence on behalf of each one listening to this ministry. Save the unsaved, heal the sick, empower the believer for service, and place the hope of Thy coming in every heart. In the name of Christ we pray. Amen.

58 — The Christ of Christmas

Isaiah, with the telescope of prophecy, peered down the corridors of time and got a clear picture of the coming Redeemer. But Isaiah saw Him emaciated, bruised, bleeding and dying. He declared that His visage was so marred He no longer resembled the sons of men. And again the prophet must have thought this maltreated person must have been suffering the stroke of God's judgement for His own misdeeds.

But then the Spirit touched him afresh and he cried, "But not so, not for His sins, He was wounded for our transgressions; He was bruised for our iniquities; the chastisement of our peace was upon Him; and with His stripes we are healed."

He was made flesh in order that He might suffer vicariously for us. "He was under the law, to redeem them who were under the law." "Having been made a curse for us, He redeemed us from the curse." "He was made in the likeness of sinful flesh, that He might condemn sin in the flesh." "He, who knew no sin, was made sin for us, that we might be made the righteousness of God in Him." And finally, "He became the Son of man, that we might become the sons of God."

The Word was made flesh in order that the eternal Son might be temporarily separated from the glory of the Father and experience the frailty of man. In Christ does the Father see our weakness, disappointments, loneliness, pain, suffering and death. He was tried in every vicissitude of life you and I can experience. Jesus came in the flesh to reveal His Heavenly Father to us. After having stayed down here on the earth for some thirty years, He said to His followers, "If you have seen me you have seen my Father."

When I consider that Jesus died for my salvation and how He manifested the Father from Heaven, my response becomes, "If God is like His Son, Jesus, then I love Him and He can have my life, my all." At this Christmas season, why not give your all to Jesus? He gave His all for you. You can experience the greatest Christmas ever if you will accept God's gift, His Son, into your heart.

Let us pray. Almighty God, I pray for those of this audience who are not saved. May this Christmas be the greatest they have ever had by receiving the Lord Jesus Christ into their hearts. In Thy name I pray. Amen.

59 — Magnificent Motherhood

On today's "Christ in the Now" broadcast, I want to deal with three things concerning motherhood. They are the endowment, the enactment, and the enduement of motherhood. First, we note the "endowment" of motherhood. There are few earthly joys to transcend that which fills a mother's heart when her baby is placed in her arms for the first time. Yet, with that joy and overwhelming love comes an inestimable sense of responsibility. As she looks into the innocent face of her baby and is overcome by the miracle of God's creation, she must realize that she has not only been a partner in bringing a new life into the world, but that she has borne a soul for all eternity.

Under the guidance of the mother, the infant becomes a personality that will never die. In every normal child there are latent possibilities for greatness, for nobility of mind and spirit, for accomplishment and honor. But in that same heart also lies those tendencies which could bring failure, sin and wretchedness. God, in His infinite wisdom, has given that tender life into the care of a mother during its early and most formative years. And much of what it will become depends upon the impressions and influences of her life and teaching during this period. Therefore, we conclude that the "endowment" of motherhood is a grave responsibility.

Secondly, we note the "enactment" of motherhood. Every true Christian mother is concerned about the spiritual welfare of her children. Many times, however, their salvation is left to a vague hope that some day they will be converted, perhaps through the influence of the Church and become Christian men and women. The enactment of "motherhood" and "parenthood" in general has the responsibility of doing what they can to lead their children to Christ. And there are three basic principles that invariably apply to all that would lead their children to become true, steadfast followers of Christ. First of all, we must be sure that our own example of Christian experience and practice is above reproach. Children are more likely to follow the ideal of what we are than of what we say. Secondly, we should try to bring our children to a personal experience of salvation at the earliest possible age. And thirdly, each mother should seek to impart to each child a positive ideal of Christianity. We know that the Christian way of life is the best and happiest way possible, and this conviction must somehow be conveyed to our children.

The third thing concerning motherhood I bring to your attention today, is the enduement to accomplish the God given responsibility of being a mother. Every mother should realize that they are utterly devoid of grace and wisdom to accomplish the great task of motherhood. Therefore, each one should look to Him who has called you to be a mother. Throughout God's word we do not find one instance where He has given someone a work to do that He has not qualified him for its accomplishment. And surely motherhood, with its eternal significance, can claim a heavy portion of divine assistance. Mothers, God alone can fit you for the molding of souls. If you despair of your own ability, then, go to God in faith knowing that you can do all things through Christ who strengthens. Lacking in wisdom, ask of God whogives to all men liberally, and upbraideth not. Failing in resource, seek Him who has promised to supply all our needs according to His riches in Glory.

In closing, let me note that no one needs God more than a mother. But on the positive side of the ledger, I feel that no one can come to the throne of grace with more confidence that she is in harmony with God's purpose than a mother can. I'm going to pray for the mothers of this audience and I ask you to bow in the presence of Christ and believe for His help and power in your life.

Almighty God, giver and sustainer of life, I pray for every mother of this audience that your Holy Spirit would touch their hearts and lives in a very special way. In Thy name I pray. Amen.

60 — The Life of Faith

When Martin Luther did penance before his conversion, he found that self-inflicted torture or good deeds would not save. He found that treacherous feelings could never be a true anchor for the soul. But, in his searching, he found the anchor that is steadfast and sure and that truth is that "the just shall live be faith." In this verse, "the just" refers to the "justified by faith." This means that the just man has been justified freely by the grace of the Lord. And we conclude from the study of the Scriptures that only the justified man can live the faith life, the life of blessing, of victory and of joy.

To the unjustified, the life of faith seems to be impractical. Such a person has depended on sight, hearing and feeling, until it is difficult for him to accept faith. Thomas doubted the fact of the resurrection. Then, Jesus stood in the midst of the disciples and offered His hands and urged Thomas to thrust his hands into His side. Thus, Thomas was given sight to bolster his faith but Jesus afterward said, "Blessed are they that have not seen, and yet have believed." From this scripture we conclude that we as believers are among the favored that, even though we have not handled the Lord with physical hands, nor seen Him with natural eyes, yet, we have believed through the truth of the word of God.

This life of faith is necessary if we are to have the victory the Lord provides for us. I have heard many say, "I was saved by faith." Others have declared, "I was healed by faith." And, I can still hear others say, "I received the infilling of the Holy Spirit by faith." Thus, we conclude that faith is pertinent to all phases of our lives because faith is the very substance of our life. Our life is a life of faith! Every physical, material, spiritual, mental and emotional need is met and supplied by virtue of our living by faith.

I ask you today, "Is there a physical need in your life? Then, faith is the answer! Are there material needs? Again, faith is the answer! Is there a spiritual lack? Let me note again that faith is the answer! We have the wonderful privilege of knowing that the Lord will provide.

Therefore, today, regardless of your need, I ask you to bow in the eternal presence of our Lord and by faith reach out to Him who is standing so near and is so desirous to meet the need of your life.

Let us pray. Almighty God, giver and sustainer of life, I bow in Thy presence on behalf of those of this audience that have needs in their lives. May they by faith reach out and grasp Thy wonderful promises. May they know the joy of 'living by faith.' In Thy name I pray. Amen.

61 — Imputed Integrity

To be baptized in the Holy Spirit is to obey the injunction of Scripture that says, "Be filled with the Spirit." The Bible further teaches that "Ye are the Temple of the Holy Ghost" and thus expresses the very breath and essence of integrity. A man or woman in any walk of life with integrity has a secure foundation upon which a life of usefulness and fruitfulness can be built. A life devoid of integrity is a rope of sand, a refuge of lies, a mirage of the desert, a sham and a broken reed at all times and under all circumstances. But to be a man or woman full of the Holy Ghost means to live a balanced life, a life of integrity, honesty and dependability.

The Apostle Paul, writing to Timothy, declares, "For God hath not given us the spirit of fear, but of power and of love and of a sound mind." I believe that this can apply to a businessman or woman in their dealings as well as an individual in his spiritual life. We live in a day when fear grips the hearts of so many people around the world. The Bible teaches that fear hath torment. But, thank God, we have not been given a spirit of fear, because the Holy Spirit gives us courage to meet all the varied and multiple responsibilities and challenges of life. But we need more than courage to live a balanced life of integrity. We need the power to back up this courage. God not only gives us courage, but He also gives us power. This is where the work of the Holy Spirit comes in. The Holy Spirit is the Spirit of Power. He is co-equal, co-eternal, and co-existent with God the Father and God the Son and as such, He is unlimited. One of the staggering and awesome marvels of the fullness of the Spirit is the coming of the omnipotent One into our lives to live; to give us power to witness and power to fulfill all of the other requirements and challenges of a dynamic, victorious and triumphant Christian life. There is no question of how much power God has; rather, it is a question of how much we will allow Him to manifest in our hearts and lives.

It is not enough, however, to have courage and even power. I have known men whom I believe had power with God, but they were far more destructive than they were constructive. Therefore, we need the great love-spirit, which oils all of life's machinery with the wonderful quality of divine love.

There is nothing that makes us more like God, act like God, feel like God and manifest the presence of God, than having the love of God shed abroad in our hearts by the Holy Ghost. This not only gives the courage for integrity and the power of integrity, but it also warms this integrity with the very heart-emotion of the living God. If one had to choose one of the manifestations of the Holy Spirit, surely this must be one of the most important; and this is to enter into the fullness of the love-spirit, which is the Holy Spirit.

At the danger of sounding repetitious, I say it is not sufficient only to have courage, power, and even love. We must have the maximum effectiveness for our God as men and women of integrity. The Scriptures delightfully declare, "God hath not given us the spirit of fear, but of power, and love and a sound mind." If anyone in the world should be truthful, upright, and be a person whose word is a bond, it is the individual full of the Holy Ghost which is the "sound mind" Spirit. Let us thank God that the Holy Spirit, who is the very spirit of truth, holiness, wisdom, knowledge and understanding, plus a thousand other marvelous characteristics, is able to make us think straight, right, proper, and with complete integrity even in the remarkable days in which we live.

Let us pray. Almighty God, Father of us all, I pray for everyone in this audience today that they might be filled with Thy wonderful Holy Spirit. In Thy name I pray. Amen.

62 — Unchanged in a Changing World

The year 1972 will bring many changes. And many times change is disturbing because of the possibility of insecurity. Yet today I would like to give you a ray of hope because there are many things that will never change. And most of these involve the crucial factors of life.

First, let us note that God the Father will never change. The Bible states that God has no shadow of turning and no variation from a set course, rule or pattern. It is impossible for Him to change. The Scriptures teach that God is sovereign and no power can compel Him to change. Because there are forces in the world greater than us, our plans become indefinite, and yet God never faces such an issue. The Bible states, "The counsel of the Lord standeth forever and the thoughts of His heart to all generations." Because God is unchanging He will be the same in the New Year as He has been in the past. He will be just as kind because His love and mercy do not change. We know that human kindness is always changing. Experience warns us that those who are kind to us today may be unkind tomorrow. But our Father's kindness is unchanging in that God has said, "I have loved thee with an everlasting love." While we are not sure that our love to God will be constant, we are certain that His love for us will never diminish at any time during 1972.

Secondly, Jesus Christ will not change in 1972. Hebrews 13:8 affirms that "Jesus Christ is the same yesterday, today and forever." Creation changes but He does not. His faithfulness will not change for He who keeps us today will not forsake us tomorrow. Because Jesus is unchangeable, His intercession for us will not slacken. His tenderness and sympathy will not change, nor shall we lose His supply of grace for Christian living. Every day of the year He will be arrested by the cry of the distressed. He will value the gift of the poor widow and put his arms of love around little children. The joy we possess is that earth's changes can but bring the unchangeable Christ closer to us.

Thirdly, God's word will not change in 1972. The Scriptures declare that "Heaven and earth shall pass away, but my words shall not pass away." Peter added that the word of the Lord endureth forever. I believe that the word of God will be in the new year what it has been in the past. It will impart to us the same comfort. It will give us hope and will continue to speak to us in daily life. In 1972 as we go on to new scenes and expanding knowledge, we shall enjoy unspeakable blessings. And as we rest our lives on what cannot be changed, we shall experience the unshakable integrity of God's promises.

Ladies and gentlemen, in the coming year this can be our personal conviction that "God is our refuge and strength, a very present help in trouble. Therefore will not we fear though the earth be removed and though the mountains be carried into the midst of the sea."

Let us pray. Almighty God, giver and sustainer of life, help us begin the new year with the conviction that You and Your Son as well as your word never changes. And from this truth may we gain strength to face the inevitables of life. In Thy name I pray. Amen.